KW-480-748

LIST OF PLATES

FOREWORD

The world's a theatre, the earth a stage
Which God and Nature do with actors fill.

THOMAS HEYWOOD.

♣ ♣ ♣

In the theatre there lies the spiritual good and
kernel of all national poetic and national moral
culture. No other branch of art can ever truly
flourish, or ever aid in cultivating the people, until
the theatre's all powerful assistance has been com-
pletely recognized and guaranteed.

—WAGNER.

♣ ♣ ♣

On the stage one must have reality, and one must
have joy. In a good play every speech should be as
fully flavoured as a nut or apple.

—JOHN MILLINGTON SYNGE.

♣ ♣ ♣

If the theatre is to hold up to us Nature's mirror,
then it must show us the good and bad in life, but
without horrifying us with the horrible or nauseat-
ing us with the salacious. The theatre is a school
and its stage is a moving power in society for good
or evil.

—DAWSON BYRNE.

xi.

THE STORY OF IRELAND'S NATIONAL THEATRE : THE ABBEY THEATRE, DUBLIN : BY DAWSON BYRNE, M.A.

THE TALBOT PRESS LIMITED
EIGHTY-NINE TALBOT STREET DUBLIN
AND CORK

FIRST PUBLISHED 1929

PRINTED IN IRELAND BY
THE TALBOT PRESS LIMITED
DUBLIN

Photo by]   [Keogh Bros., Dublin

THE ABBEY THEATRE.

To

WILLIE G. FAY
& FRANK J. FAY

the Founders
of the Irish School
of Acting

CONTENTS

THE
STORY OF IRELAND'S NATIONAL THEATRE

THE ABBEY THEATRE, DUBLIN, IRELAND.

CHAPTER I.

IRISH DRAMA IN QUEST OF A HOME.

1.—*The Irish Literary Theatre.*

ONE of the most remarkable literary and dramatic movements of modern times is associated, naturally and inevitably, with the name of the Abbey Theatre. That theatre was in a very real sense the cradle, as it has been for twenty-five years the home, of the Irish National Drama. Yet it must be remembered that much vision, much patient courage, much literary and histrionic enthusiasm, and much practical administrative skill had to be expended before that drama secured a permanent stage for its presentation.

The Abbey Theatre owes perhaps more than is generally recognized to the brothers Fay. But the

Fays themselves would be the first to admit their own debt to the inspiring influence of the little band of writers whose ambitious dream in 1898 was a distinctively Irish drama played by native actors.

In her book "Our Irish Theatre" Lady Gregory has recounted the first steps to the realization of that dream. At a country house in the county Galway she and Mr. Yeats were chatting after lunch:

"The talk turned on plays. Mr. Martyn had written two, *The Heather Field* and *Maeve*. They had been offered to London managers, and now he thought of trying to have them produced in Germany, where there seemed to be more room for new drama than in England. I said it was a pity we had no Irish theatre where such plays could be played. Mr. Yeats said that had always been a dream of his, but he had of late thought it an impossible one, for it could not at first pay its way, and there was no money to be found for such a thing in Ireland. We went on talking about it, and things seemed to grow possible as we talked, and before the end of the afternoon we had made our plan. We said we would collect money, or rather ask to have a certain sum of money guaranteed. We would take a Dublin theatre and give a performance of Mr. Martyn's *Heather Field* and one of Mr. Yeats's own plays, *The Countess Cathleen*. I offered the first guarantee of £25."

Such was the inauguration of the Irish Literary Theatre, whose not very prolific existence extended to three theatrical seasons and then terminated. The first play to be produced under its auspices was

The Countess Cathleen, on May 8, 1899. *The Heather Field* occupied the stage on the following evening. The second season opened in February 1900 with the production of George Moore's *Bending of the Bough,* succeeded by Martyn's *Maeve* and Alice Milligan's heroic drama *The Last Feast of the Fianna.* Finally, in October 1901, came two plays: *Diarmuid and Grania,* an interesting experiment in collaboration, and Douglas Hyde's *Casadh an t-Sugain (The Twisting of the Rope),* the first Gaelic play to be produced in any theatre.

Diarmuid and Grania was founded on the well-known Irish story of the lovers whose beds were the cromlechs. The dramatisation of the story is one of the curiosities of literature. George Moore, it was decided, should write the play in French, Lady Gregory translate it into English, Taidgh O'Donoghue retranslate it into Irish, and Lady Gregory again translate it into English. " You," said Moore to Yeats, " will put style on it."

The piece unfortunately did not commend itself to its audiences. There was general dissatisfaction with the effort to adjust English voices to the turns and twists of Irish idiom. The failure that resulted emphasized what had been one of the essential defects of the Irish Literary Theatre—its dependence on imported actors. Six of the seven productions which marked its brief career had been performed by English players. Only *Casadh an t-Sugain,* which shared, as we have seen, with *Diarmuid and Grania* the programme of the final season, had a native Irish cast; it was played by a company of amateurs trained by W. G. Fay. Thus, by a curious

irony, it was not till the Irish Literary Theatre was
on the point of passing from the stage of dramatic
history that it enlisted the services of the little group
of actors who were destined to do so much to make
the dream of 1898 a definite reality.

2.—*The Fays.*

While Yeats and Lady Gregory were engaged in
their heroic but losing fight to keep alive an Irish
drama, there were in Dublin a number of young
people who for the love of the thing used to spend
their evenings rehearsing and playing under the
direction of Mr. W. G. Fay and his brother Mr.
Frank J. Fay. The brothers had organized a company as the " Ormond Dramatic Society," and produced their plays in various halls in and around
the city of Dublin.

Their first efforts were confined to old time farce
which was so popular in those days: *Box and Cox,
Boots at the Swan, My Wife's Dentist, The Limerick
Boy, The Secret, His Last Legs,* and others of the
same type. W. G. Fay was a professional actor with
many years' experience; Frank J. Fay excelled as an
elocutionist and had undergone a thorough course
in the art of acting under the guidance and tuition
of a capable actress of the day. The little company
was thus in competent hands.

Farce makes highly exacting demands on the
player's technique. For that precise reason it is the
best possible medium for beginners who are really
anxious to acquire proficiency in their art. Of
traditional farce "business" W. G. Fay had at his

finger tips a wealth which he imparted unstint
to his company. Able and hard-working ac
themselves, the brothers were most critical ;
conscientious producers. It was their princi
never to present to the public anything that was
not artistically ripe for presentation, and this often
necessitated months of rehearsal for one short play.
It has been the secret of their success as producers
and managers—a success which, in view of their
wonderful work later at the Abbey and elsewhere,
no one will be disposed to deny.

3.—*Ibsen's Apprenticeship.*

The Fays' amateur dramatic company had in their
many years of playing gained a little reputation in
the city of Dublin. One eventful morning early in
1901, Frank Fay happened to take up a copy of the
London " Morning Leader"—a paper no longer in
existence—and found in it an article by William
Archer, the celebrated English scholar and critic,
entitled " Ibsen's Apprenticeship."

In 1850 there was only Norwegian drama, but no
Norwegian theatre. There was a playhouse in
Christiania, but the actors were all Danes, and the
scant theatrical entertainment of the smaller towns
was supplied by companies of Danish strollers. The
Danes were in every sense of the word foreigners ...
The separation of Norway from Denmark in 1814 had
been followed by a notable development of Norwegian nationalism in poetry, in painting, and in
music; but it was commonly regarded as hopeless
for Norway to think of possessing a drama of her
own. People had come to regard Danish as the
natural language of the stage, very much as French

is regarded as the natural language of diplomacy. Fortunately this was not the view of Ole Bull, the great Norwegian violinist. In 1849 he returned to his birthplace, Bergen, from a triumphal foreign tour, bringing back a forest of laurels and a pocketful of money. He found in Bergen a poor bare little theatre built in 1800, which had been used partly by Danish strollers but mainly by the amateur actors of the lively little town. Even amateur acting had, however, for years fallen into desuetude; so that when Bull conceived the idea of establishing a Norwegian theatre he found absolutely no material ready to his hand. There existed no such person as a Norwegian actor or actress, no such thing as a Norwegian play of the slightest merit. Even Henrik Ibsen's *Catalina* (published in the following year) was as yet only a roll of manuscript in the desk of a druggist's apprentice at Grimstad. Ole Bull, however, found a warm welcome for his idea among some of the leading citizens of Bergen.

Bull met with encouragement rather than ridicule when he inserted the following "Announcement" in local papers: —

NORWEGIAN THEATRE IN BERGEN.

Ladies and Gentlemen who wish to make a profession of singing, instrumental music, acting, and natural dancing, are offered engagements. Original dramatic and musical compositions will be accepted and paid for according to circumstances. Applications should be sent in writing, as early as possible, to

THE NORWEGIAN THEATRE IN BERGEN.

Bergen,   (Signed) OLE BULL.
23rd July, 1849.

Quaint stories are related, it need scarcely be said, of the applicants who presented themselves in answer to the advertisement; but among the very

first, by an extraordinary stroke of luck, was a boy
of seventeen named Johannes Brun, who proved to
possess a comic genius of the rarest order. The
unanimous testimony of the best judges declares
him to be the best actor Norway has yet produced,
incomparable in purely comic parts, and in
character of mingled humour and pathos. An
excellent actress, Louise Gulbrandsen, who afterwards became Brun's wife, was also among the
earliest applicants; and altogether, Bull succeeded
in getting together a company of eight men and five
women, most of them proving to have some real
talent. A private experimental performance was
given on November 30, 1849, when the programme
consisted of a comedy of Holberg's, Mozart's
Jupiter Symphony, and a monologue in the local dialect spoken by Johannes Brun. This was the nearest
approach they could achieve to Norwegian drama.
... The actual opening of the theatre took place on
January 2, 1850. Again a comedy of Holberg's was
given, with the overture to *Egmont,* the Jupiter
Symphony, and Bull's *Visit to the Saeter,* performed
by the master himself. Incredibly, pathetically
small, according to our ideas, were the material
resources of this gallant enterprise. The town of
Bergen had only 25,000 inhabitants, performances
were only given twice, or, at the outside, three times
a week; and the highest price of admission was two
shillings. What can have been attempted in the
way of scenery and costume it is hard to imagine.
Of a three-act play, produced in 1852, we read that
" the mounting which cost less than one hundred
and twenty five dollars left nothing to be desired."
... Some idea of the financial conditions of the
enterprise may be gathered from the fact that when,
in 1851, Bull applied to the Norwegian Parliament
for an annual subvention, the sum demanded (in
vain) was under three thousand dollars—less than
a single Saturday's receipts at a popular London
theatre.

But what do material limitations matter to a man

of destiny? Bull felt that the time was ripe for a
Norwegian drama, and though he had no trained
actors, a poor and scanty public, and very little
money, he determined to have the theatre swept
and garnished, and ready for the drama when it
should arrive. At the very outset, as we have seen,
he laid his hand on a genius in the person of
Johannes Brun. In his second season a Bergen
schoolgirl, Luiee Johannesen (afterwards Frau
Wolf) joined his company and rapidly developed
into an actress of the first order. And in his third
season, looking about for someone to replace the
local and temporary stage-managers whom he had
previously employed, he pitched upon a black-
bearded student at the University of Christiania,
who happened to be none other than Henrik Ibsen.
When Ibsen, five years later, returned to Christiania,
another student, somewhat younger than he, was
ready to take his place—Björnstjerne Björnson. If
Bull had had the power to create men for his
purpose, instead of merely selecting them, he could
scarcely have done better than this.[1]

Ole Bull, Björnson and Ibsen were determined to
prevent the decay of national ideals, and their plays
were at first thinly veiled propaganda. Ibsen wrote
a series of plays dealing with life in the heroic age
in Norway to teach the people what they had been,
and followed them by a series in which he satirized
the modern life of his country to convince them
that from a splendid manly race they were sinking
into a people lacking in all moral stamina. This did
not endear him to his compatriots; but the reality
of the plays, coupled with the new technique which
he employed, made him, in a few years, the
acknowledged genius of modern European Drama.

1 William Archer in The *Fortnightly Review,* Vol. LXXV.
(New series). January to June, 1904. Vol. LXXI., Old series.

The condition in Norway in Ibsen's time was very similar to that in Ireland in the eighteen-nineties. The formation of the Gaelic League by Dr. Douglas Hyde was the first attempt to stem the flood of alien ideas under which national ideals in Ireland were being swamped. Cheap printing, the rain of cheap journals of all kinds, the spread of education, made it quite evident that without help the youth of Ireland would grow up in an atmosphere in which everything Irish was looked upon as inferior. The last national literary movement had been in 1842-1848, when the Young Irelanders had written and spoken to help the people to retain the ideals of their Fatherland, but the Rising of 1867, followed by the formation of the Land League and Plan of Campaign which formed the great Irish Parliamentary Party under the leadership of Parnell, had turned the mental activity of young Ireland into political channels away from all that concerned the arts. Out of the Gaelic League came the Sinn Féin movement; for Arthur Griffith was, of all things, practical. With the ideals of Hungary in its fight for freedom from Austria as an example, he believed that without absolute freedom neither language nor art would prevent a people from perishing. Ireland began to awake to this danger, and Dublin became the centre of an agitation for an Irish Ireland that finally brought four years of war and civil war.

Archer's account of the establishment of the Norwegian Theatre by Ole Bull and his amateurs gave Frank Fay the idea that a company of Irish actors might be able to do similar work in Ireland. At this very time Frank Fay heard the fascinating story of the beginning of the Théâtre Libre which was founded in Paris by an amateur, André Antoine, early in the spring of 1807. In a small improvised playhouse on Montmartre the young man formed a company of actors for the purpose of producing four one-act plays: these were written by some of the more prominent members of the Naturalistic School. The story of Ole Bull and Antoine so impressed Frank Fay that he suggested to his brother that they should make their company of amateurs specialize in Irish plays, and W. G. consented. The Fays felt that if there was a company then the plays would be forthcoming, and in this expectation they were not disappointed. The two brothers had something in common with Ole Bull and Antoine; they were as poor in worldly wealth and, like the Norwegian and the Frenchman, they were determined, come what might, to create an Irish Theatre for Ireland.

4.—*First Visit to London.*

One day Mr. J. H. Cousins told Frank Fay that George William Russell, better known as A.E., the poet and painter, had written two acts of the story of *Deirdre* which was published in the " The All-Ireland Review." Frank Fay did not know A.E.; nevertheless he determined to call on him. A.E. received him graciously and kindly, and moreover, read to him his play. So charmed was Fay with the beauty and freshness of it that a week later he brought his brother to A.E., who again read the play. At the conclusion of the reading, W. G. told

A.E. that, if he would finish *Deirdre* it should be put into rehearsal without delay, and to this proposal A.E. immediately agreed. So delighted were the Fays that they began rehearsals before the third act was written. *Deirdre* was quite unlike anything they had previously attempted; nevertheless they were confident that they could make a success of it.

They rehearsed *Deirdre* in the hall of the old Dublin Coffee Palace in Townsend Street, Dublin (now no more), which was fitted with a small stage. It was a difficult task, but nothing could daunt the spirit or quench the fires of enthusiasm burning in the hearts of these young Thespians.

They were greatly encouraged in the task they had undertaken by the author, A.E., who, after his hard day's work, often sat and watched, with his usual patience and kindness, those young Irish actors give life to his play. " Looking back over the intervening years I can see in fancy A.E. in the old Coffee Palace Hall, Dublin, sitting in his brown overcoat, smoking his pipe, the embodiment of kindness and patience, watching us put his words into action, but rarely making a suggestion."[2]   He believed in the company and their work, and his faith was an inspiration.

The training in the playing of farce had laid a solid foundation; it had smoothed out the rough spots and prepared the way for the more serious work. The sense of humour which farce develops keeps the actor from being sloppy when pathos has to be depicted. The rehearsals of *Deirdre* were

[2] Letter

continued each night, and every small detail attended to with minute exactness. The Fays knew their work thoroughly, and were not going to take any chances.

Arrangements were made with the authorities of St. Teresa's Temperance Hall, in Clarendon Street, Dublin (which is still in existence and doing good work) to produce *Deirdre* there. W. G. Fay and A.E. set themselves to make and paint the scenery, and some ladies, especially Miss Helen Laird, now Mrs. C. Curran, who were interested, made the dresses to be worn in *Deirdre*. Mr. W. B. Yeats gave them his *Cathleen ni Houlihan,* and in this they had the advantage of the great beauty and ability of the famous Miss Maud Gonne in the title role.

Mrs. Maud Gonne McBride, twenty-five years later gives her impressions of her part in the play at that time. She writes:

Cathleen ni Houlihan was written by W. B. Yeats to help the parish dramatic movement and presented to me for Iniginide-na-hEireann of which I was the founder and president, on condition that I myself would play the title rôle. I loved the stage, but, fearing that its glamour would take me too much away from my work for Irish freedom, I had always resisted the temptation of acting myself, although in Iniginide-na-hEireann I had started a dramatic society and taught elocution and acting to its members.

Cathleen ni Houlihan seemed part of my work for Ireland; it taught me more than many meetings, and I did not hesitate to accept the leading part and for the first and only time acted myself. It did not seem to me like acting. It was terrible—and it was prophetic. I know nothing of music, but the chants came to me; as Caitlin said, I heard them "on the wind," and they have been taken down and have always been used with the play. As I was going to the hall in Clarendon Street on the first night of the play a telegram was put into my hand telling of the sudden death of one of my dearest girl-friends and fellow-workers, Ethna Carbery; it hardly added to the sadness that was on me already as I thought of "the graves to be dug to-morrow" and the terrible and glorious struggle in which we were asking all that was noblest in Ireland to join. It is indeed "a hard service they take who would help Caitlin turn the stranger out of her house"; for they go armed only with their faith and spiritual nobility to fight the Kingdom of the Devil on earth which, I have always believed, and still believe, is symbolized and materialized in the British Empire, "and many who have red cheeks will have pale cheeks," for Ireland's struggle is not ended.[3]

Mrs. Gonne McBride stated that for the first and only time she acted in *Cathleen ni Houlihan*; she was never a member of the Fays' company, and therefore must not be regarded as one of the original Irish Players. She was a beautiful lady of commanding presence and wonderful personality. I often heard her speak at open-air meetings during the Parnell political movement, and was struck with the marvellous quality of her voice. On these occasions she was accompanied by two massive Irish wolfhounds. She married Major McBride of Boer War fame, and divorced him some years later.

Mr. Stephen Gwynn, the well-known Irish writer, says of Miss Gonne: "Miss Maud Gonne, as everyone knows, is a woman of superb stature and

[3] Letter

beauty; she is said to be an orator, and she certainly has the gifts of voice and gesture. To the courage and sincerity of her acting I can pay no better tribute than to say that her entrance brought vividly to my mind a half-mad old wife in Donegal whom I have always known. She spoke in that sort of keening cadence so frequent with beggars and others in Ireland who lament their state. But for all that, tall and gaunt as she looked under her cloak, she did not look and she was not meant to look like a beggar."[4]

These two plays—*Deirdre* and *Cathleen ni Houlihan*—were produced April 2, 3, and 4, 1902. The hall was packed on each occasion, and the plays caused quite a sensation. A.E. was called before the curtain and made a vivid and thrilling speech. The joy of the little company knew no bounds. They had accomplished what seemed at first to be impossible; *Deirdre* was an assured success and they had proved that they were capable of taking up a regular line of serious Irish Drama.

Immediately Frank Fay suggested to the actors that they should continue to rehearse during the summer months, to which they readily agreed; proving in another way that he had the right material at hand for the great and glorious work they had set out to do; namely, to found an Irish National Theatre, with Irish men and women as actors, and to produce Irish plays by Irish dramatists and writers.

The company was made up of several young

[4] " An Uncommercial Theatre," in *Fortnightly Review*, p. 1052, 1902.

poets, writers, and others, who have since become famous in their chosen line. Mr. Dudley Digges has won great repute in America both as a producer and an actor. He is the guiding star of the New York Theatre Guild plays, in fact, the man behind the throne. He is regarded as one of the greatest character actors in America. Who can ever forget his magnificent portrayal of Henry Clegg in St. John G. Ervine's great play *John Ferguson,* and his Mr. Zero in Rice's superb play, *Roger Bloomer*; or his outstanding performance as The Sparrow in *Liliom,* the legendary play of Ferenz Molnar. Mr. P. J. Kelley is another Irish Player who has gained distinction on the American stage and is at present playing on Broadway with Walter Hampden, a member of whose company he has been for some years; he has also played Shakespearean rôles with Sothern and Marlowe, and J. K. Hackett. Padraic Colum, now world-famous as a writer of stories, was also an Irish player, and played in the first presentation of *Deirdre* in April 1902. Mr. J. H. Cousins, who later occupied the chair of English Literature in Tokio, and who is now the head of a large Synthetic College in the Himalayas, India, lays claim also to having been a member of Frank Fay's company, and of having played in the first production of *Deirdre,* as does Mr. Fred Ryan, who afterwards went to Cairo to edit a newspaper, and who is a philosopher and an interpreter of foreign affairs. Another member was Mr. James Starkey, who writes as Seamus O'Sullivan.

After these three performances of *Deirdre* and *Cathleen ni Houlihan,* the Fays called a meeting of the company to see if it were possible to raise money to hire a hall to rehearse in. Here were young men and women giving their time and attention after their daily work to the acting of those Irish plays, and they were sufficiently enthusiastic to pay for the privilege of doing so. To play in such a cause was a labour of love to them, and moreover they were willing to help from their scanty earnings. At this meeting each member gave what he could afford, and with this money they were able to rent a small hall in High Street, where they rehearsed throughout the summer months of 1902. From this little hall occasional visits were made to a beautiful spot near Carrickmines in the county of Dublin, popularly known as Bride's Glen, where the rehearsals were held in the open air. Among the plays rehearsed that summer were: *The Laying of the Foundations,* by Fred Ryan; *The Racing Lug* and *The Sleep of the King,* by J. H. Cousins; also *A Pot of Broth* and *The Hour Glass,* by W. B. Yeats. In the month of November 1902, at what was known as the Samhain[5] Festival, held at the Antient Concert Rooms, Great Brunswick Street, Dublin, some of these plays were acted, and *Deirdre* and *Cathleen ni Houlihan* were revived. The first performance of *The Magic Well,* by Father Dinneen, in Gaelic, was also given.

Mr. Stephen Gwynn, the well-known novelist, critic, and poet, secretary of the London Irish Literary Society, was present at the Samhain Festival performances, and within a short time

[5] Samhain (pronounced *Sow-in*), the Gaelic for Hallow Eve.

W. G. FAY.

wrote of them as follows in the " Fortnightly Review":

The Sleep of the King, a poetic play, gave the actors an opportunity of showing how they spoke what was written in metre. They spoke verse, not as actors generally do, but as poets speak it, in a kind of chant, which seems to me the natural and proper manner. It was just this quality, the absence of all stage mannerism, the willingness to speak poetry simply as poetry; to speak it for its own sake, and not to show the actor's accomplishments—that rendered possible the production of *Deirdre;* and it would have been a pity for work so good not to have been produced ... and the spectacular beauty, even on that mean stage, was considerable; the figures moving behind a gauze veil in costumes designed by the author, who is an artist as well as poet, and moving no more than was essential for the action. It was a great relief to see actors stand so still and never to have attention distracted from the person on whom it naturally fell.

Writing of *Cathleen ni Houlihan,* he says:

The actors played the piece as it was written; that is, they lessened instead of heightening the dialect and the brogue; they left the points unemphasized but they had the house thrilling. I have never known altogether what drama might be before ... wherever these plays are played they will present a wholly different order of dramatic art from that which prevails in the English theatre; wherever they are played I hope they may find actors as good as Mr. W. G. and Mr. F. J. Fay and Mr. Dudley Digges, an actor of extraordinary range. ... The entire company excelled by their absence of stage tricks so common to other actors. Such plays naturally called for a different acting technique from the ordinary play.[6]

6 Stephen Gwynn in the *Fortnightly Review,* Vol. LXXII, July to December, 1902, pp. 1048—53.

Early in 1903 the Fays and their associates formed themselves into "The Irish National Theatre Society," with W. B. Yeats as President, George William Russell (A.E.), Douglas Hyde, and Miss Maud Gonne as Vice-Presidents. Mr. Yeats's motto for the newly-formed society was that it should have no propaganda other than that of good art. Up to this period Lady Gregory had not been connected with the company, but from this time on she wrote pieces for them.

Through the influence of Mr. Stephen Gwynn, the company was invited by the Irish Literary Society in London to give two performances at Queen's Gate Hall, Kensington. To arrange this was a difficult task, as all the actors, like those of the Théâtre Libre company, were employed during the day at their various occupations; but to play in London was an opportunity not to be thrown lightly aside, so a definite date was arranged (a Saturday). The little band of players crossed to England on Friday evening, arrived in London in the early hours of Saturday morning, May 2, 1903, breakfasted at their hotel, took some needed rest, later going to the Queen's Gate Hall, where they appeared at a matinée and evening performance before a very choice and select audience made up of celebrities, among whom were Mr. Henry James and all the critics of the London Press. The latter very generously commended the players. To quote Mr. Frank Fay: " It was a nerve-racking experience to play before such people, but the plays went without a hitch ... The evening performance was as success-

ful as the matinée, but when it was over I did not
know if I was standing on my head or my feet. It
was a most wonderful experience."

On Sunday evening they returned to Dublin to
resume their ordinary and commonplace occupations on Monday morning. But this particular
Monday morning they awoke (as the saying goes) to
find themselves famous. The Press of London was
crying the praises of the plays and the players.
A. B. Walkley in the "Times" wrote: "Stendhal
said that the greatest pleasure he had ever got from
the theatre was given him by the performances of
some poor Italian strollers in a barn. The Queen's
Gate Hall, if not exactly a barn, can boast none of
the glories of the ordinary playhouse; and it was
there that only a day or two ago a little band of
Irish men and women, strangers to London and to
Londoners, gave some of us who, for our sins, are
constant frequenters of the regular playhouse, a few
moments of calm delight quite outside the range of
anything which those houses have to offer ... As a
rule they stand stock still, the speaker of the
moment is the only one who is allowed a little
gesture ... The listeners do not distract one's
attention by fussy ' stage business,' they just stay
where they are and listen. When they move it is
without premeditation, at haphazard, and even with
a little natural clumsiness as of a people who are
not conscious of being stared at in public, hence a
delightful effect of spontaneity; and in their
demeanour they had the artless impulsiveness of
children, the very thing one found so enjoyable in
another exotic affair, the performance of Sada

Yacco,[7] the Japanese actress. Add to that the scenery of Elizabethan simplicity, no more than a mere backcloth, and you will begin to see why this performance is a sight for sore eyes—eyes made sore by the perpetual movement and glitter of the ordinary stage."[8]

Mr. Walkley's statement in the foregoing, that in acting the members of the company who were not speaking just stood still and listened, refers to a principle in acting which the Fay brothers followed from the outset. Their plays were rather plays of dialogue than of action, and therefore the attention of their audience had to be concentrated on the spoken word.

The idea of enhancing scenes by continued movement of minor characters or people forming crowds on the stage began on the English stage about the time of Sir Henry Irving without regard for the dictum of the greatest English dramatist, Shakespeare, that all unnecessary movement distracts the attention of the audience. It also overlooked the fact that up to our time humanity has only developed two eyes which, under normal circumstances, work in conjunction. If therefore, other movements are made on the stage during the speech and movements of those at the moment principally engaged in the scene, it means that the audience has to look in two places at once, and by so doing loses the continuity of the spoken lines. It was against these false conventions that the Irish players fought when

7 Sada Yacco, the first Japanese woman to become an actress.

8 The London *Times*, May 8, 1903.

they reduced movement to a minimum and confined it to those actors who were immediately concerned with the scene.

Mr. Frank Fay was a great admirer of Constant Coquelin, the renowned French actor, and from the close observation of Coquelin and his actors, and from a sound reading knowledge of the dramatic literature of England and France, one can easily comprehend where Frank Fay had got his ideas. Many years afterward Frank Fay tells me that he read the following: "The audience cannot look in two places at once, the eye is such a tyrant that it distracts from the subject then necessary to be considered, directing the attention to useless and obtrusive movement. The value of repose is so great that it is difficult to estimate it. At rehearsal the amateur, having finished his speech, invariably asks of the stage manager what he shall do next. As soon as he ceases to be the interesting figure he should observe the action of the other characters; that is the most natural by-play, and the least likely to do harm. It acts like the distance in a picture, that by being subdued, gives strength to the foreground, but the tyro is generally fearful that he will fail to attract attention, whereas obscurity instead of prominence may at that very time be the most desirable. To do nothing on the stage seems quite simple, but some people never acquire this negative capacity."[9]

A great achievement of the Irish actors was their clear enunciation and the beauty of their elocution. It was full of rhythm and that infectious continuity

[9] *Autobiography of Joseph Jefferson.*

which is practised by the French actors; there was vivacity of tone and accuracy of phrase; in fact, a perfection which can have come only after years of practice. This must be attributed to Frank Fay, who had given years of study to this branch of art, and who imparted his craft to the members of the company by the practical demonstration of his own marvellous and beautiful voice. Over twenty years ago Forbes Robertson, now Sir Johnston, was known as the actor with the beautiful voice; to-day we might say the same of Frank Fay without detracting from Forbes Robertson. Mr. Yeats has on several occasions praised Frank Fay and his actors for their magnificent rendering of the lines in his own plays. The soft rhythmic speech and delicate intonation of the Irish actors has been much admired, and this wonderful quality of voice has done as much to contribute to their success as any other accomplishment.

The following letters are fitting tributes to the wonderful acting of the Fays and their pupils: —

May 10, 1903.

DEAR MR. FAY.—I have just got your address from Mr. Yeats and I want to say how much I admired and enjoyed the performance (I only saw the matinée) of your company. I am no longer writing dramatic criticism, and thus had no chance of writing about it. But I hope to recur to it some day in the future when I am saying how I think acting should be done. I need not tell you how entirely I sympathize with your general principles: the quietude and simplicity of the whole thing, the beautiful speaking, and, in the case of your brother, a real genius for acting which seems rather an instinct than an art. That means, of course, that he

is a fine artist. Your own performance of the Fool
I thought wholly admirable. Miss Walker had a
touch of genuine distinction in her reticent naturalness ... It seems almost the first time I have ever
seen a company in love with the words they spoke.
—ARTHUR SYMONS.

I was much interested in the acting yesterday. I
like the light thrown on the faces so that one can
watch the finer changes there. I like the arrested
movements at a time of emotion, as when the
peasants remain in rather violent attitudes watching
the woman's form through the door. It was like a
Greek vase. I like the quiet moving about and still
quieter resting about of the old peasant woman,
Michael's wife. The costumes seemed to me so
right because they were just settings to the speakers.
To my mind, eye, and ear, every sense, every power,
should be with the actor, with " the talking." You
are happy in the actor who took the Fool's part. I
must secure him for my own troop!! I have
several magnificent parts that he could fulfil. He
can give the impression of retaining treasure, of
keeping back secrets too wonderful to be told. I
can only say I liked being there. It is what the
disciples said on the Mount of Transfiguration. To
find it " good" to be in a place is the highest praise.
—MICHAEL FIELD.

What the Fays really did was to adapt the
principles of the best English and French acting
plays by writers who could draw character and
write dialogue. In all Antoine's productions at
the Théâtre Libre the actors, when speaking, face
each other instead of facing towards the audience
as Goethe insisted on in his rules for actors. The
Irish actors faced each other and it seemed more
natural, but the actors of the old school were
trained to stand and hold their heads in such a

position that they were partly facing each other yet the full face could be seen. The principal thing in the theatre is to be seen and heard, and the profile is never as expressive as the full face. When witnessing any of the present productions of Mr. Frank Fay, one will easily notice that the faces of the actors are visible from all parts of the theatre; facial expression is to him all-important, nor does he waste the vocal effort by sending the voice into the wings. Just as the plays staged by the Fays in the early days needed modification of the acting, so, too, the ultra-modern plays staged by Antoine required a different style of acting.

When Antoine's plays were acted outside the Théâtre Libre they were failures, because wrong methods of acting were applied to them. When Antoine himself acted with Madam Réjane he looked very much like an amateur, but when playing with his own actors who followed his lead the result was remarkable.

Frank Fay was interested in the acting of his players and spent all his energy on that phase of the theatre alone. He is essentially an actor; he does not pretend to be, nor has he ever thought of himself as, anything else—his great ambition in life was to act not in peasant plays or peasant characters but Shakespearean, and also to produce the plays of Shakespeare. This ambition of his has been gratified, for he has played in sixteen of Shakespeare's plays and produced seven or eight with more than ordinary success. He writes me: "I wanted to act. I *have* acted. I have got the knowledge of Shakespeare's plays that I wanted, and how to produce them. I should like to spend the rest of my life producing and acting in them." To Frank Fay must be attributed the discovery of some of the greatest actors and actresses of the Abbey Theatre: Mr. Arthur Sinclair, Mr. J. M. Kerrigan, Mr. Fred O'Donovan, Sara Allgood, Maire O'Neill, Maire Nic Shiubhlaigh, and many others who first won fame at the Abbey.

The following very interesting letter appeared in "The Academy," May 16, 1903:—

SIR,—Your sympathetic notice of our Irish plays and players has it that they were produced under my direction. They were produced under the direction of Mr. W. Fay, our stage manager, and Mr. Frank Fay, our teacher of speech, and by the committee of our Dramatic Society. Mr. Fay is the founder of the Society, and from the outset he and I were so agreed about first principles that no written or spoken word of mine is likely to have influenced him much. On the other hand I have learned much from him and from his brother, who knows more than any man I have ever known about the history of Speech on the Stage. Yours, etc., —W. B. YEATS.

Miss A. E. F. Horniman, who did such great work at the Gaiety Theatre, Manchester, England, was present at the performances at Queen's Gate Hall, and in an interview afterwards with Mr. Yeats she told him that, if the company could keep going for a year, she would see what could be done towards giving them a place to house their plays.

In a letter to Frank Fay Mr. Yeats said: "Now as to the future of the National Theatre Company, I read your letters to a wealthy friend who said something like this: 'Work on as best you can for a year, let us say. You should be able to persuade people during that time that you are something of a dramatist and Mr. Fay should be able to have got a little practice for his company. At the year's end do what Wagner did, and write a " Letter to My Friends " asking for capital to carry out our idea.' Now I could not get from this friend of mine whether he himself would give any large sum, but I imagine that he would do something."

5.—*The Camden Street Hall.*

In reading the history of the foundation of enterprises and of peoples who later became prosperous and famous, we are struck with their pertinacity, perseverance, and grit; and anyone who knows of the early struggles and hardships of the brothers Fay and their associates in their attempt to place their little enterprise upon a solid foundation, must know the sufferings and tortures of mind they endured. Money, money, was the whole trouble, as it was to Antoine in his attempts to establish the Théâtre Libre. Up to this none of the actors received any remuneration for their services; they were in love with their art and were only too willing to play for the love of doing it. But halls had to be rented and paid for, costumes had to be made, printing and advertising had to be done, and continual rehearsals and frequent performances were now a necessity. For all this, money was required; and where this money was to come from was a positive puzzle to every one of them. In spite of the many difficulties and handicaps, a hall was rented at 34 Lower Camden Street, Dublin. Having been untenanted for a considerable time, it was in a very dilapidated condition, and the roof was inclined to leak in wet weather. But it was the best the company could afford. It was quite bare of furniture; and, having got possession, the next question was how it could be made workable. One member discovered a foundry that had castings of iron standards for school seats, so a quantity of flooring boards were bought, and the cast-iron legs screwed on to them, and these boards utilized to build the stage. Then the proscenium was built and painted, and a friendly gasfitter erected the footlights and headlights. The girls made the curtains, and the producer painted the scenery.

In this hall *The Laying of the Foundation*, by Fred Ryan, was produced. It was a satire on the Municipal Council of Dublin, and what few Pressmen came to see it were mildly interested. One said he would have enjoyed it more if the raindrops had not fallen continually down the back of his neck. He did not know that the actors were suffering from the same kind of torment. The Hall was built at the back of a provision shop, and the next shop was a butcher's, so that on Saturday night (the only time the company had a free day for their productions) both the butcher and the provision dealer put on an extra display outside their shops for market night, and the theatre audience were compelled to squeeze their way in between long boxes of eggs and huge sides of beef. One lady was heard to exclaim, as she gathered her skirts together to enter, "Well, I've been to many theatres, but, dear me, this is quaint." Lady Gregory's first play, *Twenty-Five* was produced here, and when political work became too strenuous for Miss Gonne, and she resigned her vice-presidency of the Society, Lady Gregory was elected in her place. In this hall a few performances were given; but it was found too small, and afterwards they used it for rehearsals and for the storing of such scenery and properties as they had gathered in their short existence.

J. M. Synge's *In the Shadow of the Glen,* and Yeats's *The King's Threshold* were rehearsed there, but were produced in the Molesworth Hall in Molesworth Street, Dublin. The production of *In the Shadow of the Glen,* October 8, 1903, brought J. M. Synge into public notice and no little prestige to the Irish National Dramatic Theatre and its actors. Synge's play aroused the ire of Arthur Griffith of " The United Irishman" newspaper. On the morning of the production one of the Dublin daily newspapers, forgetting the decencies of journalism, attacked the Society, evidently on hearsay, as the editor had never seen or read the manuscript, nor had he ever seen a rehearsal. This paper seemed to be prejudiced entirely against the plays for reasons not far to seek. It did not want to see a portrayal of the genuine Irish character. It was more accustomed to seeing caricatures of the Irish at the Queen's Theatre, the Gaiety, or the Theatre Royal. The Irish-Ireland movement had made continual attacks on the comic Irishman of the English stage, and the change in thought and continual political warfare had made the national feelings very sensitive to anything that seemed to belittle the people of Ireland.

The Irishman of Lever and Lover, transported to the stage, had become out-of-date, for the free and easy life of that time amongst the peasantry had ceased to exist through the Land League battles with absentee landlords. Emigration was carrying away thousands every year, and at last Ireland was aware of the danger facing her Nationals. Dion Boucicault, who wrote the best of the Irish plays of the preceding decade—*The Colleen Bawn* and *The Shaughraun*—had taken his characters from the Lever and Lover types, but the younger generation flouted them as " stage Irishmen" and would have none of them. It is a strange fact of theatre tradition that the play-bills of the first performance of the Boucicault plays contained a statement that his plays and characters were "a protest against the stage Irishman." Evidently he did not think the stage Irishman of his day was true to type any more than the Press of Dublin did his own plays before the coming of the Irish National Theatre Society.

Like everything new the latest movement was bound to meet with opposition, and it did to a marked degree. But unfavourable criticism and obstacles served only to arouse the authors, managers, and actors to greater efforts. In fact, it was this opposition which gave them the needed impetus to do greater things. Lady Gregory made her public début as a dramatist in this year (1903) with her play *Twenty-Five,* while Yeats produced his *Hour Glass,* both pieces receiving the plaudits of large and enthusiastic audiences. From this period

Lady Gregory became actively identified with the Irish National Theatre Company. Many plays were produced this year, including another from the pen of Yeats, *The King's Threshold,* and Padraic Colum's *Broken Soil,* thus introducing three dramatists whose work brought themselves and the actors so much publicity and gave them such a note of distinction that they began to be regarded as somebodies in the world of literature and drama. Some of these plays were brought to London and played at the Royalty Theatre in March 1904; among them were: Yeats's *The King's Threshold* and *Pot of Broth;* Synge's *In the Shadow of the Glen* and *Riders to the Sea;* and Padraic Colum's *Broken Soil.* Plays and Players were received enthusiastically. The great paper " The Manchester Guardian" sent a special representative to London to report on the performances. This gentleman showed a perfect understanding of the aims of the plays and players.

The acting of the company is best spoken of as a whole. It has two exceptionally capable actors in W. G. Fay and Frank Fay, and an actress of great natural endowment in the lady who acts under the name of Maire Nic Siubhlaigh. But the chief achievement is common to the whole company ... These Irish actors have contrived to reach back past most of the futilities that have grown upon the ordinary theatre of commerce, and get a fresh, clean hold on their craft in its elements. They know how to let things alone, how to stand still when nothing is to be done in the way of enhanced artistic effects by moving; how to save up voice and gesture for rare and brief passages of real poignancy, how to fade into the background when attention has to be concentrated on a single other character.

Among the celebrities present was the delightful James H. Barrie (now Sir James), the celebrated Scotch dramatist who has no rival as a writer of sentimental comedy and is the author of numerous beautiful plays, *The Little Minister, Dear Brutus, Peter Pan, Quality Street, Admirable Crichton,* etc.

This visit to London was a most opportune and fortunate event. The little troupe of Irish actors gained the sympathy of the public, the praise of the critics, a well-deserved recognition from celebrities in the world of art, and the advantage of playing in real theatres to real theatrical audiences.

After years of struggles, hardships, and the adverse criticism of their own countrymen, the wheel of fortune had turned in their favour. The proverb "A man is not a prophet in his own country" was well verified in the case of those players, who were fighting against desperate odds for recognition, and who were trying to do something for their country in literature and drama. To lift it from the rut into which it had fallen and lain for so long was no small task. Those young Irish men and women were not at this time receiving one penny for their services, but were gladly giving their all to the cause for which they laboured. To them it was a work of love, and they were exceedingly happy, feeling assured that some day they should gain the recognition that their plays and their art deserved.

6.—*The End of the Quest.*

Their recompense did come in the person of a Miss A. E. Horniman, a lover of the theatre, who had become thoroughly acquainted and impressed with their aims and ideals since the day she was present at the performance at Queen's Gate Hall in London. Her interview on that occasion with Mr. Yeats, in which she promised to help them if they could keep going for one year, was remembered; and now this generous lady was about to fulfil that promise in a most substantial way. Miss Horniman obtained the lease of a little theatre in Dublin known as The Mechanics' Institute Theatre. She had it re-arranged and partly rebuilt at a cost of £7,000; renamed it The Abbey Theatre, and gave it to the Irish Players free of charge for a period of six years, together with an annual subsidy which was never used. Thus the Abbey Theatre became the first endowed theatre in any English-speaking country. The following extract from a Review published by the directors of the Abbey, and Miss Horniman's letter, will make a fitting end to this chapter: —

Miss Horniman has rearranged and in part rebuilt, at very considerable expense, the old Mechanics' Institute Theatre, now the Abbey Theatre, and given us the use of it without any charge. I have printed at the end of "Samhain,"[10] by Miss Horniman's request, the letter containing her offer and the company's acceptance of it; and I need not say that she has gained our gratitude, as she will gain the gratitude of our audience. The work of decoration and alteration has been done by Irishmen, and everything, with the exception of a few articles that are not made here, or not of good enough quality, has been manufactured in Ireland. The stained glass in the entrance hall is the work of Miss Sarah Purser and her apprentices, the large copper mirror frames

10 Occasional Review, from which this is taken.

FRANK J. FAY.

are from the new metal works at Youghal, and the pictures of some of our players are by an Irish artist. These details and some details of form and colour in the buildings as a whole, have been arranged by Miss Horniman herself.

Having been given the free use of this Theatre, we may look upon ourselves as the first endowed Theatre in any English-speaking country, the English-speaking countries and Venezuela being the only countries which have never endowed their theatres; but the correspondents who write for parts in our plays or posts in the Theatre at a salary are in error. We are, and must be for some time to come, content to find our work its own reward, the player giving his work, and the playwright his for nothing; and though this cannot go on always, we start our winter very cheerfully with a capital of some forty pounds. We playwrights can only thank these players, who have given us the delight of seeing our work so well performed, working with so much enthusiasm, with so much patience, that they may have found for themselves a lasting place among the artists, the only aristocracy that has never been sold in the market or seen the people rise up against it.

MISS HORNIMAN'S OFFER OF THEATRE
AND THE SOCIETY'S ACCEPTANCE.

[Copy]   H 1 Montagu Mansions,
                                        London, W.,
                                          April, 1904.

DEAR MR. YEATS,—I have a great sympathy with the artistic and dramatic aims of the Irish National Theatre Company, as publicly explained by you on various occasions. I am glad to be able to offer you my assistance in your endeavours to establish a permanent theatre in Dublin.

I am taking the Hall of the Mechanics' Institute in Abbey Street, and an adjoining building in Marlborough Street which I propose to turn into a small theatre, with a proper entrance hall, green room, and dressing rooms. As the Company will not require the Hall constantly, I propose to let it for lectures and entertainments at a rental proportionate to its seating capacity.

The Company can have the building rent free whenever they want it, for rehearsals and performances, except when it is let. They must pay for their own electric light and gas, as well as for the repair of damages done during their occupation. The building will be insured, and any additions to the lighting for special occasions or plays must be permitted by the Insurance Company formally in writing.

If any President, Vice-President, or member of the Company wants the Hall for a lecture, concert, or entertainment, the rent must be paid to me as by an ordinary person. If a lecture be given on a dramatic or theatrical subject, and the gross receipts go to the Irish National Theatre, then the President, Vice-President, or member of the Company can have the hall for nothing. But it must be advertised clearly as being for the sole benefit of the Irish National Theatre, pecuniarily, as well as in aid of its artistic objects.

The prices of the seats can be raised, of course, but not lowered, neither by the Irish National Theatre, nor by anyone who will hire the Hall.

This is to prevent cheap entertainments from being given, which would lower the letting value of the Hall. I hope to be able to arrange to number most of the seats and to sell the tickets beforehand, with a small fee for booking. The entrance to the more expensive seats will be from Marlborough Street, where there will be a cloak-room.

The situation, being near to the tramway terminus, is convenient for people living in any part of Dublin. I shall take every possible means to ensure the safety and convenience of the public. I can only afford to make a very little theatre, and it must be quite simple. You all must do the rest to make a powerful and prosperous theatre, with a high artistic ideal.

A copy of this letter will be sent to each Vice-President, and another to the Stage Manager of the Company, yours sincerely,—A. E. F. HORNIMAN.

[Copy.]   34 Lower Camden Street,
Dublin,
11th May, 1904.

DEAR MISS HORNIMAN,—We, the undersigned members of the Irish National Theatre Company, beg to thank you for the interest you have evinced in the work of the Society and for the aid you propose giving to our future work by securing a permanent theatre in Abbey Street.

We undertake to abide by all the conditions laid down in your letter to the Company, and to do our utmost to forward the objects of the Society. —W. B. YEATS; F. J. FAY; WILLIAM G. FAY; JAMES G. STARKEY; FRANK WALKER; THOMAS G. KOEHLER; HARRY F. NORMAN; HELEN S. LAIRD; GEORGE RUSSELL; MISS WALKER; ADOLPHUS WRIGHT; MISS GARVEY; VERA ESPOSITO; DORA L. ANNESLEY; GEORGE ROBERTS; DOUGLAS HYDE; J. M. SYNGE; SARA ALLGOOD; FREDERICK RYAN; PATRICK COLUM; STEPHEN GWYNN; AUGUSTA GREGORY.

CHAPTER II.

THE THEATRE ROYAL OPERA HOUSE.

1.—*Origins.*

How many who are interested in the Abbey Theatre and its plays; how many managers, dramatists, or actors, who have trod its boards and gained fame and name within its walls, know or ever cared to know anything of its history or origin? "Theatre Royal Opera House," such was its original name. It was built in the year 1820 by a Mr. Jones, familiarly called "Buck" Jones. Three or four years later it was destroyed by fire. Back in those days of the long ago, in the days when Dublin city was the Mecca of the aristocrat, when the lords and ladies of the aristocracy of Ireland had their town houses in Rutland, Mountjoy, Fitzwilliam, and Merrion Squares, when Dominick, Henrietta, and Marlborough Streets were no less great and grand; the little theatre at that time must have had some patronage from the surroundings in which it stood. The young bloods of the day must have paid it many a visit.

In the time of Ireland's prosperity it was prosperous, and in the time of its depression it was sorrowful. Like all human things it felt the ravages of time; but it weathered the storm and reared its head again to see another greater and more glorious race treading its boards and sitting within its ancient walls.

The Mechanics' Institute was at that time situated in Capel Street, Dublin. It was the rendezvous for the members of a Temperance Sodality under the direction and guidance of a priest. This priest took over the ruins of the burned theatre in Abbey Street and secured a lease of the ground for nine hundred and ninety-nine years.

A new Mechanics' Institute was erected on this ground and the "Theatre" rebuilt by public subscription, and given " In Trust" by this priest to the mechanics of Dublin as a Temperance Hall forever. The mechanics of Dublin, not being strong on the temperance question, began to drift away to more congenial and convivial surroundings; consequently, the trustees found it a difficult proposition to pay the ground rent. The building was left to the mechanics on the express conditions that it should not be let, sold, or bestowed.

However, about fifty years ago a Pat Langan, an Irish comedian, opened it under the name of The People's Music Hall, and for a number of years flourished there. We next find it in the hands of a Harry Gill, and later a Loder Lyons. Still later we find it under the management of a McNally, who did pretty well until he produced a pantomime which brought him into trouble. The theatrical proprietors and managers of the surrounding playhouses took him to court for an infringement of the law, as the theatre had no patent or licence for such a production. The fortunes of the once respectable Theatre Royal and Opera House had by this time fallen very low, and continued to fall still lower under the management of one Gaffney and a Mrs. Glenville, a once well-known character actress from the Queen's Theatre in Brunswick Street, who ran it as a Music Hall (or Vaudeville House) with the regular run of cheap artists; in fact, it was at that time more of a boxing gymnasium than a "Theatre." It had descended so low socially that no decent person would care to be seen entering there. But this little theatre, like any other place of business, needed but proper and careful management to make it a paying proposition.

2.—*Vicissitudes.*

On April 6, 1901, Mr. J. B. Carrickford and Madam Louise Grafton ventured to open its doors to the public as a dramatic house with a company composed mostly of old English stock actors. It was at this period that I became identified with the theatre. I was engaged as a juvenile actor, and as I had never previously been inside the house, my first entrance within its walls was as an actor.

Mr. Carrickford had changed the name to the National Theatre, which now seems to have been prophetic. The place had only one trustee, a man by the name of Gilmour, who kept a small shop at the corner of Abbey and Sackville Street (now O'Connell Street). The other trustee, a Henry Allen Taylor, had given up his trusteeship. The theatre was heavily in debt, a fact unknown to Mr. Carrickford, the lessee; but to his horror and amazement he soon found out, for within a few months he was served with a writ for ground rent. A copy of this document I here append, as it will doubtless be of great interest to many readers.

In the High Court of Justice
King's Bench Division

Henrietta Marie de Selby and
Henry John Allen
Writ of Summons
If the sum of £51 15s. 0d. together with £1 10s. 0d.
for costs be paid to the plaintiff or her solicitor or
known agent or receiver within ten days from the
service of this writ all future proceedings will be
stayed.

..............................Solicitor[1]

The writ was issued by Messrs. A. D. Kennedy and
Feggis of Upper Sackville Street, Dublin, solicitors
for the plaintiff who resided at 87 Boulevard
Mariette, Boulogne-Sur-Mer, France. The gentleman who served the writ informed Mr. Carrickford
that if he cared to pay the money into Mr. Kennedy,
the solicitor's hands, the building would be his.
This seemed rather absurd, nor could Mr. Carrickford for a moment believe that a theatre could be
purchased outright for the small sum of £50.
However, he had an interview with Gilmour, the
trustee, who did not know what to do and cared
less what became of the place. Eventually Mr.
Carrickford offered to pay the debt and retain the
sum advanced in weekly rent, a proposal to which
Gilmour agreed. Affairs were smoothed out in this
way and Mr. Carrickford continued with his productions. The new name and new management had, in
a very short time, wrought wonders. Large
audiences became the order and one could notice
quite a change in the quality and type. The general

[1] Solicitor in England, lawyer in the United States.

run of patron had been quay labourers, sailors from merchant and trading vessels, newsboys, street vendors, and flower girls. But the theatre, the actors, and the audience had undergone a complete change, and had taken on a tone of respectability. A very large business was done, so much so, that special police were placed on duty to handle the crowd. The actors had become favourites and had quite a following of their own.

On many occasions we had visits from the students of Trinity College, curious to see the resurrected theatre. They treated the performance with every respect, and, as they acknowledged many times, "were pleased and surprised." Anyone who knows the Trinity students and how they can cut up and wreck a place in the twinkling of an eye will realize what their patronage and approval meant. Many young ladies and gentlemen, ambitious to act, sought engagements, and were at times given small parts. All this took place within a period of two years, 1901-03, during which over three hundred plays were produced, ranging from the Elizabethan period to the modern drama of those days. Each play held the boards for but three nights, which meant constant and laborious work for the actors.

The theatre was practically our home, as we were there from 11 a.m. until 11.30 p.m., with but a short break of a few hours in the afternoon. It had never been licensed as a dramatic house, so all plays were presented as one-act plays (without cuts). This procedure was thought to keep the house within the law, but such was not the case. The success attained by Mr. Carrickford aroused the jealousy and anger

of the Queen's Theatre management, who had come
to realize that even a little theatre situated as this
was and commanding such a class of audience could
be made a success. Moreover they had become
alarmed; "the gods" had deserted the galleries of
the Queen's and had come to stay at the National;
with the result that about this time inquiries were
being instituted, old musty law-books were being
dragged from dusty and moth-eaten shelves, and
dusted and searched to find out if there was any
possible way in which the National Theatre could
be closed and put out of existence. Alas, a way was
found! The Queen's management had turned
informer, had given information to the minions of
the law at Dublin Castle (the then stronghold of
England's spies and informers) that Mr. Carrickford
was producing drama at the National, and that he
should be ousted without a moment's delay. The
penalty for such offences in those glorious days of
King Edward's reign was the insignificant sum of
£300 per night for playing drama, farce, or pantomime in any building in Dublin not holding a patent
from Dublin Castle. £300 per night! Monstrous!
Absurd!

This debt, amounting to about £270,000 (1,350,000
dollars) due to His Majesty the King of England,
should have brought Mr. Carrickford into great
notoriety; and sent him to life imprisonment. But
Sir Patrick Coll, Chief Crown Solicitor, called on
Mr. Carrickford and Madame Louise Grafton (Mrs.
Carrickford) and most graciously promised to stay
proceedings on the condition that they ceased to
run the theatre as a house of drama. This they con-

sented to do. Their only alternative was to run the house as a Music Hall or Vaudeville House, which they did, and with every success. But there was some force being brought to bear against any class of entertainment whatever. The Dublin Corporation now interfered and demanded expensive alterations, which were impossible under such uncertain conditions. A big fire with loss of life in an English town startled the municipal authorities into activity all over the Kingdom, and the Dublin Corporation, following suit, closed down the National Theatre for lack of necessary exits in fire emergency.

3.—*Transformation.*

Mr. Willie Fay, hearing that there was no possibility of the present lessees' undertaking the heavy expenses these alterations would entail, and also knowing from the construction of the building the impossibility of its being again licensed, got into communication with Miss Horniman and reminded her of her promise to help if a building could be found suitable for the Irish National Theatre Society. She came to Dublin and went into the matter with her architect, Mr. Joseph Holloway. The authorities would not consent to the reopening of the Theatre without more exits. This difficulty was overcome by her purchase of an old Penny Bank building in the next street, which had formerly been used as the City Morgue, but was abandoned some time previously owing to the erection of a new one on a more suitable site. This was too good a chance for the Press to miss, so they spread the story that "the Irish National Theatre was to be established in a Morgue, and judging by the plays they produced, it was the right place to start in." This morgue or bank building allowed a new entrance to the stalls of the theatre and provided an office and dressing rooms. Miss Horniman made tempting offers to the trustee, Gilmour, to purchase the house outright, which she did for a lump sum.

Every credit is due to Mr. J. B. Carrickford and Madame Louise Grafton for lifting this theatre from obscurity and oblivion. They catered for the poorer classes—the tenement dweller, the labourer, newsboy, flower-girls, and the flotsam and jetsam of Dublin's streets, who looked forward to their visit to this little theatre as a heaven where they could forget their sorrow and the sordidness of their lives, at least for a few hours, to live in the land of romance. But they attracted also the educated class who at one time had ignored this house and looked upon it as fit only for the scum of the slums.

It is now the Abbey Theatre. Ye gods, what a change! What a transformation! This theatre of the Dublin slums has regained the glory of its former days of one hundred years ago. It is now one of the greatest repertory theatres in the world, where the aristocrat, the student of literature and art, sit side by side with the working man and woman to enjoy the plays of Lady Gregory, Yeats, Synge, T. C. Murray, George Shiels, William Boyle, Lennox Robinson, Padraic Colum, once in a while Shaw, and lately of that genius of the slums, Sean

O'Casey, who has written of his own kind and has placed them on the Abbey stage, laying bare their faults and failings, their joys and sorrows—and who could do it better than he, for is he not himself a child of Dublin's slums?

CHAPTER III.

THE ABBEY OPENS.

In this theatre they has plays
On us, and high up people comes
And pays to see things playing here
They'd scat and run from in the slums.

1.—*A Pen Picture.*

THE Abbey Theatre is situated in the lower half of Abbey Street, on the corner and lower half of Marlborough Street, and adjacent to the famous river Liffey which runs through the centre of Dublin. It is about four hundred yards from the Customs House.

The Abbey Theatre derives its name from the street in which it stands, which in turn derives its name from St. Mary's Abbey, an old monastery or convent which existed in the Cromwellian days and which, indeed, Cromwell may have destroyed. It is now the oldest theatre in Dublin. The Abbey Street portion is built of brick, the Marlborough Street portion of gray stone. This gray stone building —the old Penny Bank (or Dublin Morgue if you so prefer it)—is now rebuilt, painted, and decorated in a very becoming manner and makes a splendid and imposing main entrance. From this entrance one gains access to the orchestra seats or stalls, also the balcony. The entrance in Abbey Street, which was

45

formerly the main entrance, leads down some steps to the pit. The theatre is built in horse-shoe style and can seat five hundred and sixty-two people. There are no boxes at the sides as in other theatres. The stage in height and width is in proportion to the size of the house. There is no great depth, only about fifteen feet, owing to an alley-way running at the back. In the alley-way is situated the entrance to the stage, dressing-rooms, and manager's office. The lighting system is unique, specially arranged foot and head reflectors throwing a soft glow of light on the stage, entirely in keeping with the atmosphere of the plays.

The seats are not upholstered but are covered with red leather; they are anything but luxurious; nevertheless, they are comfortable. The ceiling is very high; the supporting walls are painted a dull red with a shield or coat of arms as the only decoration. The walls, ceiling, and gallery are the original ones. The orchestra is situated in front of the stage without rail or barrier of any kind separating musicians and audience; the music is mostly classical, and wonderfully played under the direction of Dr. J. F. Larchet. The act drop or curtain is a black background with gold stripes. The most peculiar and interesting feature is the deep-toned gong, which echoes through the house thrice as a warning that the play is about to begin.

2.—*Cathleen Ni Houlihan.*

It is the opening night, Tuesday, December 27,

1904, and the Abbey Theatre is making its début. It is about to recreate Ireland, to put upon its stage plays that are to represent Irish life and Irish lore, of mystical idealism and loveliness. The house is darkened, musicians disappear, the curtains are parted, all light is focussed on the stage—the play is on. In this atmosphere one sits enthralled, full of excitement, wonder, and expectation; soon one hears the voices of the actors vibrate through the theatre, and one realizes that he is listening to a strange language, yet most harmonious and beautiful.

The play is *Cathleen ni Houlihan,* full of tragedy and pathos, and one begins to live as it were in an enchanted land; so enraptured does one sit that there is not a thought of the world outside. The scene takes place in a little cottage near Killala in the home of Peter and Bridget Gillane, whose son, Michael, is going to marry Delia Cahel, the daughter of a rich farmer. Peter and Bridget have a younger son, Patrick, a fine sturdy lad. Bridget, the mother, is arranging Michael's wedding clothes, and old Peter, with the heart of a miser, is chuckling to himself and counting over in his mind the one hundred bright guineas that he is to receive from Delia Cahel as a dowry for his son Michael. The whole family is rejoicing, the young lovers are thinking only of their future joy and happiness, the light of love is shining in their eyes; they are building air castles and making their plans. The family of Gillanes is Ireland, resigned to its fate, crouched and bound in the bonds of slavery.

Outside are heard again and again the sounds of distant cheering. Patrick runs out to learn the cause, and Michael goes to the window. Looking out he sees an old woman coming towards the house with pale and sorrowful-looking face. She looks through the window and Michael shivers with an unknown dread, and says to his mother, "I'd sooner a stranger not to come to the house the night before the wedding." But his mother bids him open the door, and in walks the old woman and seats herself by the fire. The old people question her and she speaks of her travels on the road, saying that sometimes her feet are tired and her hands are quiet, but that there is no quiet or rest in her heart. She speaks of troubles and the land that was taken from her, her four beautiful green fields, meaning Ulster, Leinster, Munster, and Connacht, or the whole of Ireland. She chants in a subdued tone, while rocking herself as the old Irish women do when in grief or lamentation:

> "I will go cry with the women,
> For yellow-haired Donough is dead,
> With a hempen rope for a neck-cloth,
> And a white cloth on his head."

The sound of her mournful chant attracts Michael, who becomes fascinated by it. He asks her many questions, and she tells him of the men that died for love of her. The old people offer her food and money, but she refuses it with scorn, saying: "If any man would give me help, he must give me himself, he must give me all." Michael,

DUDLEY DIGGES.

under the old woman's spell, is about to go with her, when his mother interposes and says, "Maybe you don't know, ma'am, that my son is going to be married to-morrow. Nor did you tell us your name." The old woman replies: "There are some that call me old woman, and some that call me Cathleen ni Houlihan. They that had red cheeks will have pale cheeks for my sake; and, for all that, they will think they are well paid." She departs, chanting her weird song, leaving Michael open-mouthed and spell-bound, and his mother attempts to arouse him. The door is thrown open and Patrick bursts into the room, shouting, "There are ships in the bay, the French are landing in Killala." Michael hears the chant of Cathleen ni Houlihan outside, it is ringing in his ears and calling to him. His bride clings to him, but he dashes her aside and rushes out, leaving his father, mother, brother, and his heart's beloved. Then old Peter asks Patrick: "Did you see an old woman going down the path?" And Patrick replies: "I did not, but I saw a young girl and she had the walk of a queen." These last words brought forth thunderous applause that could be heard far away like the shouts of the young men when the French landed at Killala. It stirred up the blood of the young Irishmen, so that I thought they would never cease cheering. The sight was inspiring and thrilling, and one felt carried away as if marching along the road with troops of Irish volunteers while they sang to the music of their band, which played "God Save Ireland."

Cathleen Ni Houlihan.

Oh, the cabin's long deserted, olden
      memories awake—
Oh, the pleasant, pleasant places; hush,
      the blackbird on the brake,
Oh, the dear and kindly voices; now their
      hearts are fain to ache.

They are going, going, going, and we
      cannot bid them stay;
The fields are now the stranger's, where
      the stranger's cattle stray,
Oh, Cathleen ni Houlihan, your way's a
      thorny way.

—Ethna Carbery.

The opening programme included *On Baile's Strand,* by W. B. Yeats, *Spreading the News,* by Lady Gregory, and *In the Shadow of the Glen,* by J. M. Synge. Two of the players of this opening night have since become as world-renowned as the Abbey Theatre itself. I refer to Sara Allgood and Arthur Sinclair.

CHAPTER IV.

THE ABBEY PLAYERS ON TOUR AND AT HOME.

IN November 1905 the company journeyed again to England, and played at Oxford and Cambridge, whence they went to St. George's Hall, London. They presented Synge's *Well of the Saints* and *In the Shadow of the Glen,* Lady Gregory's *Spreading the News,* Yeats's *On Baile's Strand* and *Cathleen ni Houlihan,* Padraic Colum's *The Land,* and W. Boyle's *Building Fund.* Mr. Arthur Symons the eminent critic, paid a well-deserved compliment to the acting of the Fays in Colum's play, *The Land.* Of the latter he writes: "Its simplicity is so subtle that one is surprised to find how well it comes over the footlights. Here, no doubt, much is due to the acting, which added nothing but interpreted, and especially to the highly finished art of Mr. F. Fay and the inimitable comic genius of Mr. W. G. Fay. You [he was writing to E. J. T. Green, the English author and critic], I know, will bring notice to these astonishing people whom the English artists are beginning to find (what do you call it?) 'clever.' They do not seem to me clever at all; it is we who have clever actors; but one of these men can bring beauty upon the stage and the other can bring life."[1]

[1] *Sunday Times,* Dec. 3, 1905.

On April 16, 1906, the players produced Lady Gregory's translation of Molière's *Le Médecin Malgré Lui*. The Fays were anxious to include the "business," movement, and positions that have come down from Molière and are preserved at the Comédie Française, Paris; and with the assistance of an acting edition published by M. Jules Truffier, then sociétaire of the Comédie, they succeeded in doing so.

The following letter will, I feel sure, interest my readers:—

What I mean about your acting not being amateurish is this: that you, all of you, show technical skill and understand the art of impersonation, of standing still, of listening, of playing up to each other, of getting quickly on and off the stage. Now, when I saw Antoine's company over here [London] they were amateurs probably by intention, under the mistaken idea that being realistic it was fine art. But to speak slovenly and without inflection of voice, to stand in any position you fancy just because it is done so in real life, forgetting that the picture frame or " l'optique de théâtre" makes real movement seem unnatural from the auditorium— this sort of art which one so often finds outside of the professional stage and which I have the greatest dislike for, was never for a moment to be detected in the performance I saw at the Abbey Theatre ... A fine dramatic instinct, alertness, resourcefulness, subtlety—these qualities which may be ones that are innate in every member of your company, make you artists and not amateurs. But having these fine instincts you never forget that your art consists in presentation and that you are before an audience who have to be kept spellbound by your technique and moved mentally and physically by what you say and how you say it.

This letter from a world-famous London producer confirms what the "Manchester Guardian" critic had written, and shows what four years' careful training in the best principles of acting had achieved. It is quoted because it is the opinion of an expert, and also because it disposes of statements that "the players were quiet and natural because they did not know what else to do. They had not learned to go wrong." The players did what they did because they were trained to do it. Acting is not reality, but a convention of selected tones, gestures, and movements by the skilled use of which an effect of seeming reality may be sent over the footlights, but the convention must be mastered before that effect can be conveyed, and the above letter shows that it was mastered. As Coquelin used to say at rehearsal : "C'est pas la nature ça."

Even the apostle of what is called realism, André Antoine, knew that before one can act one must learn one's métier. In his souvenirs he writes: " I wanted to get a closer view of the great actors who fired me with enthusiasm. I enlisted under the banner of old Masquillier, the great comedian, and played in the entire repertoire with eyes and ears open to gather in everything that was going on in the big playhouses. Thus my vocation as an actor was being mysteriously worked out." Even with all this practice he laments his feeble voice and lack of métier in his Théâtre Libre days as he had not a conservatory training.

In the same year Manchester was visited with great success, also Liverpool, Leeds, and the Theatre

Royal, Cardiff, where I find the following criticism: —

I found myself at the theatre in a curious mood last night, wondering how the Irish Players would present on the stage the Celtic temperament. The names of the writers of the plays were a guarantee of literary charm and merit, but it so frequently happens that the finest and most subtly charming literature is impossible on the stage. There was a strangeness over everything because all the customary tricks and trappings of the showman's art were absent, and we were given four pictures of Irish life. The simplicity and restraint of the authors and actors explain the strength and interest of each production. One would criticise the acting of the various members of the company, but there is no standard by which to judge their efforts, except that of Irish life, and their naturalness and restraint speak success.[2]

The following theatres were also played: Her Majesty's Theatre, Aberdeen; King's Theatre, Glasgow; Lyceum Theatre, Edinburgh; Tyne Theatre, Newcastle-on-Tyne. The Glasgow appearances were very favourably received, and I quote the following as proof: —

The Irish Players at the King's Theatre, Glasgow.

Delightful Composition of Irish Dramatic Art.

It is no exaggeration to say that from the standpoint of histrionic art their visit to this city is the theatrical event of the season, if not, indeed, of our generation. This seems excessive praise, but it can be made good. Author, playwright, and actor unite in telling us that their mission in life is to

[2] Theatre Royal, Cardiff, May 29, 1906.

hold the mirror up to nature; as to the acting it is not acting at all, it is simply the people we know, doing and saying the things we may see them do and hear them say in their native villages. There are no stage mannerisms, no playing to the gallery; no recognition of the audience in any shape or form. It is the highest form of art which effectually conceals its art. Nothing like it has been seen in the country before and nothing ever has been seen like it by the writer save the playing of Molière's comedy *L'Avare* by the famous company of the Théâtre Française in Paris, twenty-five years ago.[3]

At Newcastle-on-Tyne, Frank Fay met one whom he had admired at a distance on the stage and with whose writings and acting he had been familiar, and this person was none other than Constant Coquelin, the great French actor, who was playing a matinée performance at the same theatre. Coquelin was at this time sixty-five years old, but full of life and vigour and love for his art. It was a pleasure to watch this wonderful actor in his greatest rôle, Cyrano de Bergerac.

From Newcastle-on-Tyne they journeyed to Hull, and finished a tour which brought them much success and gave them a better understanding of the theatre, a much-needed confidence in themselves, and a certainty of touch.

[3] *Glasgow Observer*, June 9, 1906.

CHAPTER V.

THE PLAYBOY OF THE WESTERN WORLD.

1.—In Dublin.

THEY now returned to Dublin where nothing of great importance took place until the year 1907, when the Abbey Theatre reached artistic heights with the production of *The Playboy of the Western World,* by J. M. Synge. This play came like a bolt from the sky—it shocked the country from Fair Head in Antrim to Mizen Head in Cork. Not in the history of the theatre had there ever been such excitement. The newspapers printed flaring headlines denouncing *The Playboy* and demanding its withdrawal, but the management stuck to their guns, refused absolutely to do so, and continued the play throughout the entire week. Immense crowds gathered to see the play and make a terrific uproar during the performances. One could not hear the actors; the audience kept up a continuous howling, growling, hooting, and hissing; some made hideous noises with tin trumpets, but despite the maddening din the actors continued to play. The disturbance was by no means confined to the interior of the theatre. In the parlance of the man in the street, a regular "free for all" went on outside, hundreds of policemen were vainly endeavouring to dispel the crowd, but found it a hopeless task. It was this play of Synge's that brought the Abbey Theatre into the spotlight of the world, made it popular and set it on a solid footing which it has ever since maintained. Previous to *The Playboy* a particular class, the educated and the " highbrow" were the only patrons. Up to this period the ordinary gallery theatre-goer would not think of patronizing the Abbey. This was a great loss to the box-office, as all theatres depend to a very great extent on the patronage of the gallery. Not only is their money useful, but their whole-hearted approval and applause gives the actor a very necessary stimulus.

The actor does not depend on the applause of the élite or educated " highbrow"; he appreciates their silent approval, which is about all they ever give. This class of theatre-goer sits through a play in an attitude of stony indifference. The difference between the " highbrow" and the occupant of the gallery is very marked. The one goes to the theatre, the other goes to the play.

Miss Horniman, who still held the reins of power, thought the players needed some professional guidance and instruction, and with this end in view brought over Mr. Ben Iden Payne from England. Mr. Payne was trained in the performance of Shakespeare and the classic drama in Sir Frank Benson's company, and had quite a reputation in England. I asked Mr. Payne to give me his impressions of the Abbey Theatre, its directors and actors. The following is his reply: —

" I have been taken like a bird or a fish." " I have
been taken like a bird or a fish." From behind the
scenery I hear the repetitions of the words emerging
from the semi-darkness in grotesque antiphony; one
voice from the black orchestra, clear, resonant, full-
toned; its echo on the dimly lighted stage,
unmodulated, flat, and hesitant. "Frank Fay teaching diction to one of the lesser members of the
company," explains W. B. Yeats It is my introduction to the inner workings of the Abbey Theatre.

The night before I had been present at the opening
performance of *The Playboy of the Western World,*
and had seen the audience (emotionally stirred by
the tragic pathos of *Riders to the Sea,* and hence
wholly out of key at the moment with the ironic
comedy of the later play) after a long, simmering
period of sporadic exclamations of opposition, boil
over into a howling chorus of execration. That had
been my introduction to the public representations
of the Abbey Theatre company.

The next day, after long discussion at the Nassau
Hotel, the directors, Lady Gregory, W. B. Yeats, and
J. M. Synge, a little bewildered but wholly defiant,
decided to go on with the performances no matter
how riotous the audience, and even if the theatre
had to be half-filled with police. Yeats had been the
most resolute spokesman for the militant policy, and
I remember how much I admired the far-sightedness
of his assurance that it was imperative they should
assert their right at all costs to produce what they
believed in as good art, or be forever dictated to by
mob-prejudice. And I remember thinking that the
audience, incomprehensible as their opposition to
The Playboy was to my English understanding, must
be peculiarly vital or it could not have expressed
its prejudice so violently.

I had arrived at this not very opportune moment
to look over the ground in order that it might be
decided whether or not I was to take up the position
—a somewhat anomalous position, as it turned out—
which had been tentatively offered, and which was

called, if I remember rightly, general manager, but which was certainly unlike anything that term usually connotes.

So began my brief connection—it lasted only for a matter of six months or so—with the Abbey Theatre. I was imported from England at the instance of Miss A. E. F. Horniman, with a view to off-setting certain criticisms levelled against the actors on the score of " amateurishness," and for the purpose of giving a " more professional tone" to the productions. It soon developed, however, that the chief, and indeed the only possible accusations of amateurishness rested upon comparatively trivial points of the most external nature, such as the careless dressing of wigs and what not. Moreover, with the characteristic compromise by which I found that all relations between company and directors, and Miss Horniman, were carried on, it had been agreed that the new general manager was to have no say in regard to the peasant plays, which occupied probably nine-tenths of the performances. It was felt, and rightly, that an English producer, trained in an alien technique, could not but damage that national quality the development of which was the pride and purpose of the organization. In practice it turned out that, as an actor first and foremost, I found myself naturally taking the side of the actors in most matters of controversy even when I felt they were poor advocates for themselves, as they frequently were.

Nor did it surprise or annoy me under the circumstances when there was, in the few poetic plays I was able to produce, little reciprocity from the actors, but on the contrary a form of passive resistance. I soon found that, rather than sink into absolute inactivity, I was allowing myself to degenerate into a mere business-manager, a position for which I had neither inclination nor capacity, and which was not the function for which I had been engaged. So I resigned.

Brief as my tenure of office had been, it had been

intimate and revelatory. My puzzlement at the opposition to *The Playboy* was not lessened by the discovery that the audiences as a rule were scanty and apathetic. A disposition on all sides in the theatre to procrastinate and to dally with work until eleventh hour necessity compelled concentration, was much out of harmony with my idea of professionalism. An atmosphere where suspicion and intrigue seemed ever vaguely emerging could not but make one uneasy. Yet, behind all, there was a freedom from the curse of commercialism which was inspiring.

I ask myself what was the strongest impression I carried away. It may be the prejudice of the actor recognizing his own, but I find in retrospect even to-day that my warmest feelings of reciprocity and understanding were mainly with the actors, those fine, instinctive artists, Frank and Willie Fay, Sara Allgood and Maire O'Neill, Sinclair, Kerrigan, and the rest. In spite of Lady Gregory's facile pen and amusing gift for peasant farce; in spite of Yeats's keenly intellectual interest in the theatre, his critical acumen, and the loveliness of his poetry; even in spite of Synge's genius, for he was a sick man working under sentence of death, I still feel that it was the actors—paying all deference, of course, to their dependence upon the written word—to whom the theatre owed most of its vitality, even as they were individually, the most genuinely enamoured of the theatre. They were seeking no interest in the theatre; the theatre had sought and found them. They were in the theatre, and of the theatre; the hunted and not the hunters, they had been taken like a bird or a fish.[1]

Mr. Payne did some wonderful work during his short stay at the Abbey. He produced Maeterlinck's *Interior*, and made of it a superb production. Miss

[1] Ben Iden Payne, Director of Drama, Carnegie Institute of Technology, Pittsburgh, Penn., U.S.A.   May 25, 1927.

Sara Allgood played the mother and made a great success in the part. Mr. Payne recognized at once that Miss Allgood was an actress of exceptional ability, but Mr. Yeats seemed loath to acknowledge the fact, so much so, that he sent over to England and engaged a Miss Daragh, an English actress, to play the part of Deirdre in the play of that name by himself.

The production of *Deirdre* was a history-making moment in the Abbey. Numerous critics were on hand to mar or make it. Miss Daragh spoke blank verse in the old English way, while Miss Sara Allgood, who was playing Lavarcham, the first musician, spoke blank verse as Mr. Frank Fay had taught her. The papers on the following morning said that the only one who spoke Yeats's verse as it should be spoken was Miss Sara Allgood. So much for Miss Daragh of England and W. B. Yeats's judgment.

Nevertheless, in spite of this, when *Deirdre* was revived, Yeats again engaged an English actress, Miss Mona Limerick, the wife of Mr. Ben Iden Payne. The most interesting point about these two imported actresses was that both had been trained in Sir Beerbohm Tree's Acting Academy, and both spoke and acted exactly alike. There was nothing creative about their work, it was just mere rule of thumb; whereas the players at the Abbey were always allowed to interpret their parts in their own way, which has made them great creative artists.

2.—*In Great Britain.*

Mr. Payne made a very agreeable and favourable impression among the Abbey Players, and they have nothing but praise for him and his work. After this experience they went on tour, visiting Birmingham, where the "Daily Post" wrote a glowing tribute which reads in part: "One gained rather the impression of actuality than of mere stage presentation." Oxford was next visited, and there *The Playboy of the Western World* was put on at the New Theatre.

Some of the Oxford critics write of their appearance:—

Pathos and humour alternated at the New Theatre on Monday night, when the National Theatre Society from the Abbey Theatre, Dublin, presented a repertoire of Irish plays. The venture was something of a novelty for an Oxford audience. The style of acting was different to anything we have been accustomed to, and the staging and scenic effects were very different to those used in an English play. Quite as much for the educational value as for the novelty is the venture deserving of success.[2]

Later the company went to the Great Queen Street Theatre, London. On this first night there was only a slight demonstration against *The Playboy,* but on the second an uproar such as is rarely witnessed in a London theatre. So violent indeed were the interruptions as to call for the interference of the police. The mental process by which Irishmen lashed themselves into a fury over a mere play puzzled while it amused English critics. One of them writes:

2 The *Oxford Times,* June 8, 1907.

The experience of last night tends to show that there are Irishmen, even in London, who are as incapable of common sense as of artistic observation. While the players were speaking dialogue which to English ears was perfectly innocent, they hissed like steam engines, and in the last act from all parts of the house came frequent storms of groans, cries of " Shame," counter-cries of " Geese" from some spectators who wanted to follow the play, and forcible remarks to the players from at least one man in the stalls, who rose to his feet and displayed symptoms of a weak mind labouring under strong emotion. And what was it all about? Neither politics nor morality. Political questions have no part or lot in *The Playboy;* there is nothing from beginning to end which can be construed into a political allusion. What the dissentient spectators groaned over was simply the wickedness of Mr. Synge in representing Irish peasants as capable of making a hero of a man who had killed his father; of glorifying a man of action, even though his action should have taken the form of parricide. That the man has not killed his father, but boasts valiantly that he has done so, is a minor matter which does not alter the essential spirit of the situation. Mr. Synge has hit on a grimly comic idea; makes of it a fine comedy and is howled down by his fellow Irishmen because he fails to paint Ireland as the home of lofty and undefiled imagination. There is no more reason to complain of him than there would be to complain of Mr. Pinero [now Sir Arthur Wing] for libelling the British aristocracy by *The Gay Lord Quex,* or hiss Mr. Barrie [now Sir James] because in the *Admirable Crichton* he chooses a member of the House of Lords as a type of incapacity for practical labour. Mr. Synge has done what every play writer worth his salt must needs do. If he writes what the Irishmen would apparently like him to write, he will allow none of his Irish characters to behave otherwise than as angels. They must be immaculate.   If he wants foolish characters they must be English.   The scene at the Great Queen Street Theatre is a striking manifestation of Irish facility in distortion.   The interrupters cannot realize the value of self-criticism.   Playboys themselves, they want playthings . . .[3]

After their very mixed reception in London the players returned to Ireland and played Cork, Kilkenny, and Waterford.

[3] The *Evening Standard* and *St. James's Gazette,* June 15, 1907.

Photo by]] [Brooks, Washington

REV. DAWSON BYRNE, M.A.

CHAPTER VI.

FROM THE PARTING OF THE FAYS TO THE DEATH OF SYNGE.

1.—*Exeunt the Fays.*

IN the early part of 1908 W. G. Fay, who was producer, manager, and leading comedian of the company, asked Mr. Yeats to give him the authority which every theatrical manager insists on—absolute control of his actors; in other words, Mr. Fay wished to make a stipulation that Mr. Yeats should dismiss the company and let them be re-engaged personally with Mr. Fay. Mr. Yeats refused to make any such concession. The Abbey directors then called a meeting in the theatre, and as no arrangement agreeable or suitable to Mr. W. G. Fay could be arrived at he chose to resign, taking with him his wife, Miss Brigit Dempsey, his brother, Mr. Frank Fay, and Mr. Ernest Vaughan; the latter had come to the Abbey from the melodramatic stage. This was the parting of the ways.

The company at this time was their first and only one, but they had intended to organize a company to play high comedy and old masterpieces, and a special company of speakers to play verse plays. They also wanted to link up with Cork and Belfast, and to interchange plays and companies from time to time. Mr. Yeats held that actors did not need teaching, but the test of over twenty years has disproved this theory, for since the theatre lost its original teachers it has never produced artists who made a world-wide reputation like those of the original company: Sara Allgood, Maire O'Neill, and Arthur Sinclair.

After Mr. W. G. Fay's resignation he went to London with his wife, and within a month he was on his way to New York to play under Mr. Charles Frohman's management, for Sir James Barrie had interested him in their work and he had engaged the Fays and W. G's wife to open at the old Savoy Theatre in 34th Street, playing *The Rising of the Moon* as a curtain-raiser to *Twenty Days in the Shade,* in which the beautiful and clever actress, Pauline Frederick, was starring at the time.

The following very interesting interview with the Fays appeared about that time:

Irish Actors tell the Dangers of Playacting in Ireland, and say that Dramatic Talent runs Wild in the Streets of Dublin.
Hard-Working Actors.

"It was hard work at the start; we had to fight for everything, but an Irishman, you know, doesn't mind a fight, so we found it very interesting and pleasant the greater share of the time. Most of the workers worked from eight to ten hours at one job or another—some in shops, some in offices, and then came to the theatre three nights a week to rehearse plays. We gave three performances a month, and after a time the theatre was able to pay a few of the actors a little something." Mr. Fay, being asked if he was ever short of actors, replied, " No, indeed;

dramatic talent runs wild in the streets; we never had to look for actors, but we were always careful to take them from the working classes. The upper ten ape the English accent, they are not themselves, and therefore they cannot act. We always selected young men and women who sprung from the peasant class, every one of them can act native drama, but the women are quicker at it.

"In Ireland it is every poor young man's business to go to work, and therefore he has little time for the less sordid side of life. The women are nearer the other things; we could get more out of an Irish girl in eighteen months than we could out of a man in two years. The girls are more natural, the men are inclined to act. They all want to be Martin Harveys." [Martin Harvey was then the rage in his play *The Only Way*, a dramatization of Charles Dickens's "Tale of Two Cities."

Miss Brigit Dempsey said: "We are satisfied to be Irish and nothing more. I was surprised when I got here to be told that it might be better for me to drop the name Bridget. I was informed that Bridget was a name associated with servants, but I decline to drop it. I'm Irish and I'll keep my name, but the Irish way of spelling it is Brigid. We're nothing if not Irish."

Mr. Frank Fay on being interrogated replied: "To deal with peasant life we must be simple. Peasants and aristocrats are the only people who are simple. They have nothing to worry about; the aristocrat has so much that he has nothing to bother him, and the peasant hasn't anything so it's the same way with him. The peasant is down to the earth, you can't knock him any further, and he is, therefore, close to the life of Ireland. The life of cities is merely commercial life. Every country that wants a native drama must go to the country for it, it is not to be found in the city. A National Theatre must draw its life from the country. We are first of all interested in native drama; we use the Irish accent to express Ireland; when we are playing we try to forget everything but Ireland. We have been taught to ignore the audience, and that has had at least one result, it has taken the conceit out of us."[1]

At the close of this New York engagement Mr. W. G. Fay and his wife returned to London and played with Sir Herbert Beerbohm Tree at His Majesty's Theatre in *The O'Flynn*. Since then he has played with most of the star managers. He produced plays continually for fourteen companies during the great World War. He then managed and produced for Mrs. Edward Compton at her Repertory Theatre, Nottingham, and at the new try-out house at Kew.

Later he produced for Sir Barry Jackson's famous Birmingham Repertory Theatre, where was staged for the first time (among many plays extending over a period of fourteen years) *The Farmer's Wife,* by Eden Phillpotts, which ran for three years at the Court Theatre, London.

From the opening night of the Abbey in 1904 up to 1906 the audiences were very small. The theatre was just struggling along, and it was dull, plodding, up-hill work all the way, and all the time. Large audiences did see *The Playboy,* but that was for just one week.

When the Fays left the Abbey, Miss Allgood, by request of the directors, took over charge of the company. This was a weighty responsibility for one so young and inexperienced. But "fools rush in where angels fear to tread," and as Miss Allgood herself remarks, " It was the arrogance of my

1 The *Evening World Daily Magazine,* Feb. 22, 1908.

ignorance that prompted me to take upon myself
such a position." However, the step was taken, and
the company stood by her, and everything looked
rosy for a time. The theatre was to open in a short
time with a new play by W. F. Casey. Everything
was set for the rehearsals when they discovered they
were minus a leading man (the Fays had always
played the leading rôles). Several were tried out,
but none were capable of filling the bill. It was
within a week of the production when some friend
gave Miss Allgood the name of a young man known
as " The Boy Preacher." He was sent for and given
the part to read and acquitted himself magnificently.
He was asked if he would care to play the part, and
he willingly agreed.

2.—*Enter Fred O'Donovan.*

Mr. W. A. Henderson was secretary and manager
of the Abbey at this time. The Abbey re-opened
again in 1908 with the play *The Man Who Missed
the Tide, by* W. F. Casey. It was a tremendous
success, and the Boy Preacher, who is no other
than the renowned Fred O'Donovan, made quite a
hit on the night of his début. *The Piper,* by Norreys
Connell, was produced the same night. The company worked loyally with Miss Allgood for about
three months, then little disagreements began to
crop up here and there with this one or that one
until Miss Allgood thought discretion the better part
of valour, quitted the job, and took up her old place
in the rank and file of the players. There may not
be found any record of Miss Allgood's name con-

nected with the management of the company either on playbills or programmes, but this is entirely due to Miss Allgood's modesty, as she objected absolutely to having her name printed as one in such a capacity. But in going through the records I found such to be a fact and express a wish here that Miss Sara Allgood will let this stand as history.

This was the turning-point for the Abbey financially, as the *Playboy* had been the artistic turning-point the previous year. I think one might safely say that the theatre reached the zenith of its success at this particular time. During this year the company remained at the theatre and added the following to their repertoire:—*The Suburban Groove,* by W. F. Casey; *The Piedish,* by George Fitzmaurice; *The Workhouse Ward*; *Teja,* a translation from Duderman; *The Rogueries of Scapin,* a translation from Molière's play, by Lady Gregory; *The Piper,* by Norreys Connell; *The Scheming Lieutenant,* by Richard Brinsley Sheridan; *The Golden Helmet,* by W. B. Yeats; and *When the Dawn is Come,* by Thomas MacDonagh, who was afterwards killed in the Irish Rebellion of 1916.

Mr. MacDonagh calls his play a tragedy, but it has more of hope than of woe. The hero dies, but the Ireland he dies for lives—is free " When the Dawn is Come!" It is, I think, the first Sinn Féin drama I have ever seen. It is the first to proclaim that Ireland will yet by her own strength and of her own will drive out the foreign ruler. It is a manifestation of the spirit which cares much for the hope of to-morrow, and little for the sorrows or heroisms of yesterday. Valued solely on its dramatic merits, *When the Dawn is Come* is the best piece produced in the Abbey in two years.[2]

At this time special performances were given for the British Association, and on each occasion the house was packed to the doors—it was completely sold out.

While playing at the Theatre Royal, Dublin, in 1907, Mrs. Patrick Campbell, the celebrated London actress, had attended a performance at the Abbey. The theatre, its actors, and atmosphere pleased her so much that she expressed a wish to play there. The play that appealed to her most was W. B. Yeats's *Deirdre*, and naturally the part of Deirdre. Arrangements were made for her appearance in *Deirdre*, in which she played the name part to the King Conchubar of Arthur Sinclair and the First Musician of Sara Allgood. Mrs. Patrick Campbell seems to have thought more of Sara Allgood's acting that she did of her own, and praises her work:

I do not know anybody at the present moment who could take the part which Miss Allgood plays in *Deirdre*, and I shall ask the Abbey management to lend me Miss Allgood for some matinées of the play in London. It seems to me a rôle which only an Irish girl could play; it is the part of a pure, warm woman. If an English actress takes such a part she is very cold, but Miss Allgood's acting has nothing frigid about it, and my belief is that warmth and purity combined is only to be had in Ireland.

Later on in November and December Mrs. P. Campbell did produce *Deirdre*, and Sara Allgood

2 The *Peasant* and the *Irishman*, Oct. 24, 1908.

again played the part of First Musician which had won such praise from the distinguished English actress. Writing of this production the " Pall Mall Gazette" says: " Deirdre was a dream worth having; anything more beautiful than the appearance and the voice of Mrs. Patrick Campbell has not charmed our senses since we saw her in another and very different play."

The Abbey Players, as they are now termed, paid a visit to Belfast, where they had an enthusiastic reception. Sara Allgood's portrayal of Maurya, in *Riders to the Sea,* made a particularly deep impression on Northern audiences.

It remains in the mind [writes one of those who saw it] as the most tragic presentation of old age that one has seen on the stage. In this bowed figure are expressed the immemorial sufferings of all who live and die by the sea, and the broken sentences are charged with an intensity of emotion that takes the spectator by the throat. The sheer art of the thing escapes one in the face of its naturalness, and when the curtain drops at last one's first feeling is that of relief. It is only then that one can estimate at something like its true value the genius of the actress. While she is on the stage one is not in a theatre, but a couple of hundred miles away on the desolate western seaboard, with the din of the breakers in one's ears and the sorrow that is the heritage of generations of fisher-folk tugging at one's heart-strings.[3]

The following by William Archer, the famous critic, will make a fitting close to the season of 1908 : —

3 The *Northern Whig,* Dec. 4, 1908.

I felt I must on no account neglect this opportunity of visiting the first endowed theatre in the English-speaking world. I saw a delightful performance of Lady Gregory's *Workhouse Ward*. At least I have seen one play performed at a theatre within the British Isles founded and conducted in a spirit of pure artistic enthusiasm.

The whole establishment seemed to me like a busy little hive of earnest workers, incomparably more stimulating and inspiring than the dead-alive stage regions of a fashionable London theatre during the triumphant run of some popular triviality. A company of artists keeping fresh, and now and then adding to, a delightfully original and eminently national little literature.

I say that the Abbey Theatre is the most admirable enterprise of its kind at present existing in Western Europe. The Irish enterprise is really finer than the Norwegian [the Bergen Theatre of which Ibsen was the manager]. We can have nothing but admiring gratitude for the delicate little literature of poetry, of humour, of national character-study, and interpretation.

Mr. Archer selects some of Mr. Yeats's plays as " among the most exquisite things produced by any living poet"; and some of Mr. Synge's as " priceless admissions to English literature."[4]

3.—*The Death of Synge.*

The year 1909 turned out to be as remarkable and successful as the preceding year. Some performances were given at the Abbey; then came a visit to Miss Horniman's Gaiety Theatre, Manchester, opening in a whole repertoire of plays. In May of this year,

[4] The *Evening Telegraph,* Dublin, Dec. 7, 1908.

after a lapse of two years, J. M. Synge's *The Playboy of the Western World* was revived at the Abbey to tumultuous applause.   This is rather astonishing when one recalls the outbursts of disapproval and fighting at its first appearance in 1907.

There is an old saying that "times change and people with them," and we see it typified in the audience which seemed to view *The Playboy* in a different light and let him go on his way unmolested.

Synge at this time was racing fast against death, which was soon to overtake him.   The early years of hardship had sapped much of his vigour and strength.   The terrible opposition to his works did not add in any way to his comfort.   Through all these years he was in failing health, and the ravages of the dread disease had done their work on the frail body.   In 1909 he went to a private hospital in Dublin, where he became much worse.   The angel of death hovered around, and, after a short time of waiting, she knocked at the door of his room and beckoned him to come.   He called the nurse and said to her, "It's no use fighting with death, I must give up," then turned his face to the wall and followed death into the unknown land from which no traveller ever returns.   John Millington Synge had passed away from this vale of tears into the valley of death to meet his Creator face to face on the 24th day of March, 1909.   Requiescat in Pace!

CHAPTER VII.

JOHN MILLINGTON SYNGE—A REVIEW.

BY Synge's death at the early age of thirty-eight the world lost one of its great dramatists. It will be appropriate here to make a brief survey of his life's work.

Born in Dublin in 1871, Synge graduated at Trinity College, Dublin, and thereafter spent some years in travel and in miscellaneous journalism. It was by the advice of W. B. Yeats, who met him in Paris in 1898, and was quick to recognize his latent powers, that he returned to Ireland to spend six weeks in the Aran Islands, remote from books and the conventional life of cities. There he studied with penetrating and observant eye the curiously picturesque life of the islanders, their stern struggle for a poor subsistence, their racy speech with its Anglo-Irish idiom, their unsophisticated outlook, and the mingled humour and pathos of a primitive civilization untouched by industrialism. In this western outpost of Europe he found something he had missed in his wanderings on the Continent. He found, moreover, as Yeats had confidently predicted he would—himself. Some of the fruits of his discoveries and experiences are to be seen in his book " The Aran Islands," which, however, did not find a publisher till 1907.

It was not necessary for the public to wait till 1907 for an opportunity of tasting Synge's genius. He challenged attention on October 8, 1903, with his one-act play *In the Shadow of the Glen,* which when staged in the Molesworth Hall was greeted with angry surprise as a brutal travesty of the Irish character. *Riders to the Sea,* another one-act play, but a singularly beautiful one which evoked no hostility, followed in 1904. To this period also, in all probability, belongs the two-act *Tinker's Wedding,* though it was not published till 1907.

Synge now essayed for the first time a long drama. This was the three-act *Well of the Saints,* which had its première on February 4, 1905. It is a story of two blind beggars named Martin and Mary Doul, who have spent the best part of their lives sitting at the cross-roads. They have never seen each other's face, and in their fancy think that they are beautiful. A longing for sight possesses them—that they may see the birds which they only know by their song, and the green fields and flowers which they can only judge by their perfume. One day a wandering smith known to them by the name of Timmy tells them that a holy friar who carries with him water from a holy well which can cure all diseases, is to pass by the crossroads at which they sit. The Saint does come and blesses their eyes with the holy water, and their sight is restored. The poor beggars behold each other for the first time, and all their dreams of beauty and loveliness fade. As time passes their eyesight again grows dim, and they are glad that it is so. The Saint returns and is about to anoint again their eyes with the holy water when the old man, Martin Doul, dashes the holy water vessel from the hands of the Saint.

Mr. George Moore at this time wrote in eloquent terms of the plays and players:

I should like to call the attention of the readers of the "Irish Times" to an important event which has just happened in Dublin, and which very likely may be overlooked by them and to their great regret hereafter. The event I allude to is of exceeding rarity, it happens occasionally in Paris. I have never seen in London any play written originally in English that I can look upon as dramatic literature. I have not forgotten Oscar Wilde's plays; that delicious comedy, *The Importance of Being Earnest*. But however much I admire them, I cannot forget their style is derived from that of the Restoration Comedy, whereas Mr. Synge's little play seems to me to be of a new growth; its apparent orthodoxy reminds us of the painters who worked in the latter half of the fifteenth century. Filippo Lippi and Botticelli did not accept religious superstition as easily as the Monk of Fiesole. There are the points of comparison between Mr. Synge's writing and these pictures, but I must reserve my explanation for another occasion. In your paper I would call attention to the abundance of the beauty of the dialogue, to the fact that one listened to it as one listens to music, charmed by the inevitableness of the words and the ease with which phrase is linked with phrase. At every moment the dialogue seems to lose itself, but it finds its way out. Mr. Synge has also discovered great literature in barbarous idiom as gold is discovered in quartz, and to do such a thing is a great literary achievement. The interpretation partakes of this literary quality; it is original and it is like itself. Mr. W. Fay was wholly admirable as the blind beggar; he was whimsical, insolent, and pathetic in turn; he was always in the key and his love scene with Molly Byrne seemed to me a little triumph of distinguished acting. The close of the act was especially effective in intonation and gesture.

Mr. Frank Fay was very good as the Saint; the part is a difficult one, and the ecclesiastical note might not have been caught as well by another actor. The part of the blind beggar-woman was so well played by Miss Vernon that I am afraid I shall regret having spoken of it for I shall not find words wherewith to praise it enough. Above all, I admired her reticence, and it seemed to me that she must have thought the part out from end to end, omitting nothing that might be included, including nothing that might be omitted. The age of the old woman is portrayed in every gesture, the walk, and the bodily stiffness, and something of the mind of the old woman, for in her voice there is a certain mental stiffness. Her elocution was faultless, some will say that she was not effective enough when she left the church, but I do not share that opinion. I think in seeking to be effective she would be less true.—Yours, etc., GEORGE MOORE.[1]

Such praise coming from the pen of as great a writer as Mr. Moore is, to say the least, very remarkable. He is, perhaps, the greatest living stylist in the English language. It takes a genius such as he is to transform ordinary words into magnificent English. The most commonplace words will, under his pen, take on a beauty that beggars description. George Moore is the author of "A Mummer's Wife," "The Lake," "The Brook Kerith," "Esther Waters," "Heloise and Abelard," "Ulick and Soracha," "Hail and Farewell," and many other books.

His play, *The Making of an Immortal*, dealing with the Bacon and Shakespeare age-old contro-

1 George Moore, 4 Ely Place, Dublin, Feb. 8, 1905.

versy, has had a wonderful reception in London, and has brought him the fame he fought for and sought to win for forty years. He says: "It seems strange to me that after forty years of hard work, boycotting, and spurning, I should, through one short play, suddenly become one of the idols of the English public. Congratulations have poured upon me, but I am only a very weak old man barely able to stand." Moore's age is seventy-six. Many people are of the opinion that Moore was connected with the Abbey Theatre, but he never had anything to do with it.

It is curious that Synge, so highly praised by W. B. Yeats and George Moore as a dramatist, should have written to Mr. Frank Fay as follows:—

Archer seems to criticize at least our prose plays as dramas first and literature afterwards. The whole interest of our movement is that our little plays try to be literature first and plays afterwards, that is, to be personal, sincere, and beautiful—and dramas afterwards.

The following is in the same letter:—"I am very well, but in an agony of horror over my play with the blind people; it is exceedingly difficult to make it work out."

Of *The Playboy of the Western World* (1907), and its reception in Dublin and Great Britain, enough has been said in an earlier chapter. Synge's last play—the unfinished *Deirdre of the Sorrows*—was produced in 1910.

It is not a little strange that one of the least militant of men—"a silent, drifting man," as he has been described—should have done more than any other to challenge Irish popular sentiment from the stage and to provoke a controversy unexampled for its bitterness in the annals of the Abbey Theatre.

The real cause of the trouble with the first Synge plays was that he had grown up in the school of Zola and Ibsen, who were both realists, and painted in monotone to get by that means a cumulative effect. They were determined to draw attention to the defects of civilization by dealing with life raw. Life was not romance to them, but " red in tooth and claw." That they were right was proved by the chaos and destruction of the Great War. They were not concerned with whether their characters were typical or not; it was effect not causes they dealt with. Synge saw material in Irish life rich in dramatic possibilities from the modern point of view, and Ibsen had discovered a new technique of play construction which he could use. Dublin had never seen a modern play except Sir Herbert Tree's productions of *An Enemy of the People,* which completely bemused them. When *In the Shadow of the Glen* was first performed they just went mad, as the London critics did when Ibsen was let loose upon them, and the pretty things they said made a very amusing book when collected by George Bernard Shaw.

Synge was not concerned with whether his characters were typical Irishmen. They were not. The new method did not deal with types—it dealt with the forces that make types. He wanted to portray the effect on four human beings of living miles from a town, up in the mountains, without human society, breeding and rearing animals in

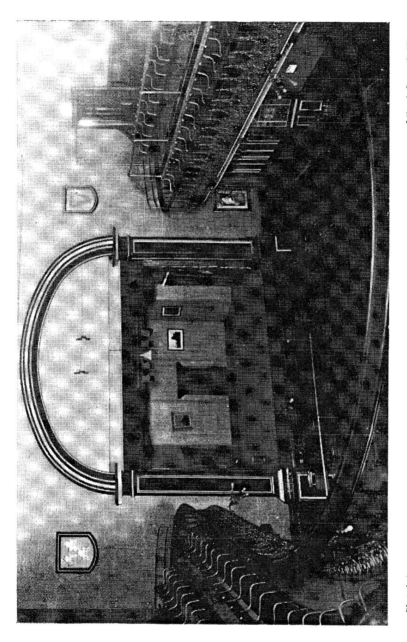

THE ABBEY STAGE.

wild, lonesome country, "where the mist would be coming up and coming down." He wrote *In the Shadow of the Glen*. It will be true in any country where there are these conditions of life. He was dealing with effects, not story-telling. That he used Irish characters for his play was for the obvious reason that he knew most about them. The public wanted romance; they wanted the Irish character depicted with a nimbus and wings despite the fact that the stage is not the place for portraying the perfect man, but the average. All new movements in the Arts are first crucified, then deified, and Time in the long run gives them their proper place in the scheme of things.

Synge said once that the drama, like the symphony, does not teach or prove anything. And contemning the plays that have one sort of propaganda or another, he spoke joyously of the best plays of Ben Jonson and Molière, that "can no more go out of fashion than the blackberries on the hedges." Being so little anxious to prescribe for the revolution in the soul of man, Synge is in danger of being underestimated by people who expect drama to be a "criticism of life," and want to leave the theatre saying: "And the moral of that is..." He takes no account of such shocking morality, such prurient idealism.

Yet I do not feel that there is anything unreal, or unconcerned about the women and men in Synge's plays. In their lives, as in yours and mine, there are hard material conditions, and if they were wise with the wisdom of this "age of reasons and purposes" they would give us pointers on the conservation of national resources, the municipalization of street railways, the sterilization of habitual criminals. But Synge has found little of wild and superb reality in these estimable topics. Instead, he writes a little play like *In the Shadow of the Glen,* that has not an opinion in it, nor a purpose in it—nothing but the emotions of everyday living, the thoughts of a woman on growing old, the gray lonesome thoughts of a fine woman married to a wheezy old man, the angry and painful thoughts of the old man, the words of a callow lover who thinks he owns the woman, the words of a tramp who paints for her, in words that sing with the beauty and illusion of freedom, the "grand evening" of the happy wanderer, and the fine songs she'll be hearing when the sun goes up.

You may read that play twenty times, and you will find that it wears like gold. It is a marvellous play with fierce humour, gallantry of image, pungent realism. Here is the wild and superb reality of our common nature, with nothing to show it off, in the lonely farmer's cottage at the head of a long glen, where all one sees are "the mists rolling down the bay, and the mists again, and they rolling up the bog."[2]

Synge's plays are vivid with realism, and throb with the life of the Irish peasant of the west. In the preface of *The Playboy* he tells us: "I have used one or two words only that I have not heard among the country people of Ireland, or spoken in my own nursery before I could read the newspapers. I borrowed the expressions from shepherds and fishermen of the west coast of Ireland, even from the beggars and ballad singers of Dublin's streets."

Art must be true to life, and Synge has been true to his art. He acknowledges and congratulates himself that he was born in Ireland among a people rich in imagination and language. For him the last

[2] Francis Hackett in "Horizons," from *Theatre Arts Monthly,* Vol. III., Jan., 1919, No. 1.

speech in a good play should be as delightful as the first. In Ireland, he wrote, "we have an ardent, wonderful, tender, and popular imagination, so much so, that those among us who wish to write start with chances that are lacking to those that write in other places, where the springtime of local life has long since been forgotten and where the harvest is but a memory, and where there is no longer straw but bricks."

When listening to the characters speaking in any of his plays, one soon realizes that one is listening to the naive and picturesque language of the Irish peasant; the originality and delightfulness of the expressions make the comic passages irresistible, while in other circumstances they impart to the dialogue a natural poetry of such piercing sadness as can never be forgotten. To be a good dramatist requires sincerity, creative genius, and ability; Synge has all these qualities in a marked degree. In his works one finds that wonderful blending of poetry and realism; his plays possess an extraordinary fascination; although the characters at times appear excessively brutal, yet there is a mingling of the beautiful with the ugly which saves them from becoming repulsive.

In all his plays he strikes the highest pitch immediately; there is no gradual working up to a climax; he does not give you time to form conclusions; he forms them for you, he is too quick for his audience. One cannot say to oneself with certainty what the climax of any of his plays will be, he keeps one on the alert from the first to the last act; one is, as it were, held breathless in suspense. The best example of this one finds in *Riders to the Sea*—a masterpiece of dramatic tragedy. This play holds you in thrall from beginning to end.

The writers and dramatists of Ireland of the past fifty or sixty years were accustomed to make of their characters caricatures. The Irish plays of Dion Boucicault, Hubert O'Grady, J. W. Whitbred, and others, of necessity, had always the rollicking Irish comedian, Conn the Shaughran, or the cringing informer, Danny Mann type. True characters, yet to-day, when the Irish man or woman is portrayed as he should be by such writers and dramatists as Padraic Colum, Synge, Yeats, Seán O'Casey, Lady Gregory, W. Boyle, Lennox Robinson, and others, a howl goes up from the four corners of Ireland. These dramatists were born and reared among the people of Ireland, and they know what they are writing and dramatizing. They know their countrymen and women, and it is this knowledge that helps them to draw their characters so true to life. All characters on the stage must, of necessity, be idealized, but not too far overdrawn either way. If in some plays Synge and O'Casey have erred in this regard, why all the lamentations, howlings, and fault-findings?

We are told by critics that Synge, Yeats, and O'Casey have not written Irish drama. What have they written? Yeats has given us the Irish fairy tale which we have heard related thousands of times all through the country of Ireland, and which we have read in magazines and periodicals, which has held us fascinated and which we have let pass without comment. But as soon as the very same fairy tale is put upon the stage of the Abbey, a cry goes forth from the ultra-refined and educated that such productions should be forbidden as a display of Ireland's superstition and ignorance; that these plays are holding the Irish up to the ridicule of the world. Supposing Mr. Yeats dramatized the Tipperary tragedy of thirty years or more ago where a father, mother, husband, and brother roasted a young woman on the iron laths of a bed, thinking, in their ignorance and superstition, that if they burned alive this frail, delicate young woman the witch by whom she was possessed would depart through the door or window in the shape of a white horse. This terrible tragedy took place in Tipperary, Ireland, and the perpetrators were sent to prison for periods of ten to twenty years. But Yeats has not yet gone so far in his characterization of Irish life, and yet the country's litterati are tearing him to pieces. If Yeats, Synge, Casey, and others have invented characters in their plays, we should be thankful for such men, for it takes a genius to create. The Irish people have been asleep long enough, and it is about time to wake them from their lethargy.

Without wishing to detract from the work of Synge, it must be said, in all truth, that he had little regard for religion or the religious life of the people of whom he wrote. He utterly disregarded the profound love of the Irish for their priests and their Church. If he wanted to write a play it seemed to matter little whom he should characterize and in what manner. We get an instance of this in the

Tinker's Wedding (first performance 1909). This was essentially the reason for the unfavourable reception of all his plays.

The Tinker's Wedding is absolute farce; the wandering tinker is always thinking of having her marriage regularized by the priest in the Church, the husband grudgingly gives his consent, and the priest of the village where their cart comes to a halt consents, after lengthy bargainings, to marry them for the fairest price of ten shillings and a tin can which the tinker is about to finish. The tinker's mother, who is an habitual drunkard, steals the can and sells it for drink. The next day at the Church door the priest refuses to marry them and they beat him up, finally covering him with a sack from which they later release him after much tormenting. The priest pretends to call down the judgments of God upon them as they run away in fear.

The characters are clear and, in a sense, true to the life of the wandering tinker, but the plot is rather absurd and far-fetched. Tinkers have a most profound respect for the priests of Ireland, and it seems beyond all comprehension that such a thing could ever happen. The whole thing is farce, and must be accepted as such. In a farce someone must be held up to ridicule; in this case it happened to be a priest, which shows very bad taste on the part of Synge. He tries to make his audience laugh at the expense of religion, and to show his countrymen their follies and failings in Nature's mirror. His satire is bitter and cruel: his characters are at times repulsive, ferocious, profane, vigorous; but human and real, though often a trifle exaggerated.

CHAPTER VIII.

FORWARD!

In June the players went over to the Court Theatre, London, for one week, then to the New Theatre, Oxford, and returned again to the Court Theatre for three weeks. It was at this time that Mrs. Patrick Campbell again played *Deirdre*. Sara Allgood, Maire O'Neill, Arthur Sinclair, Fred O'Donovan, and J. M. Kerrigan were in the cast.

During Horse Show Week, about August or September, they played the Abbey with *The Playboy,* and then produced the play that caused so much criticism at the time, *The Shewing Up of Blanco Posnet,* by George Bernard Shaw, which was banned by the English play censor, who is the Lord Chamberlain. The very fact of attempting to produce *Blanco* caused quite a mild sensation. The critics from the London and English provincial papers were sent over—in fact one may truthfully say that they came from the length and breadth of the land, eager to make a scoop with thrills of the production. But the only thrill that *Blanco* gave was to the author and the actors who played to a sold-out house and to a salvo of cheers and applause. *Blanco* was played and replayed many times. It was taken to Belfast, where it repeated its triumphs in the same sensational and very gratifying manner.

Again they crossed to Manchester, but with *The Playboy,* and then paid a return visit to London with the now sensational *Blanco Posnet.* The company gave three special performances at the Aldwych Theatre under the auspices of the Stage Society, playing *Cathleen ni Houlihan, The Workhouse Ward,* and *Blanco Posnet,* which could not be touched by the censor. At the close of the last of these performances on the Monday matinée, the company made a hurried departure for Cork, Ireland, and did not arrive there until Tuesday morning at 11.30, tired and worn-out by the sea voyage and long train journey from Dublin. Nevertheless, they played that night in Cork's fair city made famous by the song of " The Shandon Bells." They did the week there, then back to " dear old dirty Dublin," the Abbey, home and loved ones, for the Christmas of 1909.

In a popular sense, the production of *Blanco Posnet* was perhaps the most remarkable event of the year we have just reviewed. But from an artistic point of view far more importance attaches to the advent in this year of a new dramatist, Lord Dunsany, whose *Glittering Gate* was the first of a succession of plays original and unusual in conception, and, though written in prose, essentially poetic in their high imaginative power.

The year 1910 was a repetition somewhat of the previous one with the usual profitable and enjoyable season at the Court Theatre, London. Patrons of the Court were as eager for the Abbey Players' season as the players themselves.

The subsidy granted to the Abbey Theatre by

Miss Horniman for a period of six years was to terminate at the end of this year. Fully aware of this, Lady Gregory and Mr. W. B. Yeats made an appeal for subscriptions for the Abbey which met with a very generous and open-handed response from certain people in England and Ireland. A certain and evidently sufficient sum was paid to Miss Horniman, who then handed over the Abbey Theatre to the directors. To Miss Horniman of Manchester every praise is due, for it is this generous lady that made the Abbey a possibility.

When the directors were applying for a renewal of the license for the theatre, there was no little trouble with a few of the actors who had seceded from it in 1908; among them was Miss Maire Nic Shiubhlaigh. This band of players formed a company of their own under the title of " The Theatre of Ireland." Lady Gregory had kindly allowed them to play for a week or two at the Abbey on occasion, but at some time they fulfilled an engagement at the Gaiety Theatre, Dublin, in a play entitled *The Turn of the Road,* and had themselves billed as the Abbey Players. Lady Gregory naturally was offended, and thereafter absolutely refused them the use of the Abbey. And now that a renewal of the license was being sought the Theatre of Ireland Players sought to have a clause inserted that would give them the right and privilege to use the theatre at certain stated times for their plays, but their case was thrown out of court.

Realizing that the use of the Abbey was lost to them forever, they engaged a school in Hardwicke Street for their next play. This venture did not

succeed or pay so it went the way of all life's
failures, and the Theatre of Ireland passed out of
existence.

By this time the fame of the Abbey Theatre, its
authors, plays, and players was spreading in many
lands and its story being written in many languages.
The eyes of the world, theatrically and artistically
speaking, were focussed on the little theatre in
Abbey Street, Dublin. It had in these few years of
struggle and strife, taken its place among the
theatres of the world. " Forward" was the motto of
Lady Gregory, W. B. Yeats, and their associates;
forward, always and ever forward.

The most notable event of this year was the
production of *Deirdre of the Sorrows,* by J. M.
Synge, written for Miss Maire O'Neill, who is the
distinguished sister of the world-renowned Sara
Allgood. She first came into prominence when she
played Pegeen in *The Playboy of the Western World*
in 1907. In 1912 Mr. George Alexander secured her
services for the part of Zerlina in the cast of
Turandot. In the following year she was engaged
by Sir Herbert Tree to play Nerissa in his production
of *The Merchant of Venice,* in which the beautiful
Miss Julia Neilson Terry played Portia. Miss O'Neill
herself played Portia in Paris to the Shylock of
Michael Sherbrook and the Bassanio of Basil Hallam,
who afterwards became very prominent on the
London stage, but who was later killed in France
during the World War. She also played in G. B.
Shaw's play *How She Lied to Her Husband.* She
made a trip to America to play Mary Ellen in
General John Regan opposite Arnold Daly. Return-

ing to London she again played Portia with the French company at the Court Theatre. Her next prominent part was that of Lady Wishfort in Congreve's *Way of the World,* in which the now famous Miss Sybil Thorndike played the small part of the maid. Another part essayed by Miss O'Neill was that of Anna in D'Annunzio's *City of the Dead,* in which the nurse was played by Miss Edith Evans, now a very prominent actress in London.

Miss O'Neill is regarded as one of the geniuses of the stage; there is a fascination about her that commands attention. She never seems to act; everything she does on the stage is so complete with naturalness and grace, be the character a lady of the highest rank or a street hawker or tenement dweller, they take on a smoothness and dignity that baffles description.

One point that I have discovered about this distinguished actress is that she is reluctant to speak about herself or her achievements, so if she seems to be neglected in this book it is due entirely to her own reticence.

CHAPTER IX.

THE ABBEY PLAYERS' FIRST VISIT TO AMERICA.

1.—Boston.

THE year 1911 was an eventful one. In the month of May the company was invited by Mr. (now Sir) Frank Benson to play at Shakespeare's Memorial Theatre, Stratford-on-Avon, during the annual Shakespearian Festival. To act at Stratford has been, since the days of David Garrick, a coveted honour. The Abbey Players accepted the invitation, and presented the *Playboy*, Yeats's *Deirdre*, and several of Lady Gregory's plays in Shakespeare's Theatre.

It was in October of this year that the company made its memorable first visit to America, opening the newly-built Plymouth Theatre in Boston with Synge's *Playboy,* which occasioned much excitement, and supplied the newspapers with a good deal of sensational copy.

One enterprising journal, "The Boston Globe," went to the trouble of securing a committee of five representative Bostonians to witness the first production of the play in America and to pronounce judgment on it. These gentlemen approached their task with a serious sense of responsibility, and recorded their impressions in the columns of the "Globe" next morning. Three of the five condemned the play outright as being brutal, unnatural, and grotesquely untrue to the Irish character. The fourth considered it not clever enough to appeal to ordinary Irishmen. Only the fifth had a good word to say of it, finding in Synge " a great artist and a man of imagery."

Ordinary playgoers, for the most part, enjoyed the performance. There was, it is true, a certain amount of hissing, and several members of the audience found themselves in such enthusiastic disagreement with Synge's drama that they chose to curtail their evening's entertainment and walk out of the theatre. But it is safe to say that the play was a success. Yeats and Lady Gregory, who were both present on this opening night, received many congratulations on the company's excellent performance, and in the fortnight which they spent in Boston the players won the hearts of their audiences, who enjoyed to the full Lady Gregory's fresh ingenuous comedies, Yeats's ethereal but intensely human *Cathleen ni Houlihan,* Murray's powerful and sombre *Birthright,* and Lennox Robinson's two tragical satires *Harvest* and *The Crossroads.*

The acting in these and in *The Playboy* impressed all unprejudiced critics. The Irish players, it was observed, imparted to their work a unity that was both singular and beautiful, a simplicity almost unknown on the American stage. With them, movement was not everything; repose was a great deal more. To stand still upon the stage, when you would stand still in real life: that was the lesson they taught to the nervous, restless, hurrying stage managers of America. They proved that the nearest approach to life, both in its spirit and its letter, is the best art as well as the best entertainment.

2.—*New York.*

Taking Providence on their way, the company passed on to New York, where in the Maxine Elliott Theatre, a somewhat electric atmosphere was again experienced. The performance of Synge's *Playboy* evoked a disapproval that expressed itself in groans and hisses and flying potatoes. In the exuberance of their feelings, excited men and women, richly clad, threw eggs at the actors, and were ignominiously torn from their seats and ejected. It is even reported that gunmen waited outside the stage door to wreak vengeance on the players, who had to make their way to their homes under police protection.

As usual, however, the objectors, for all their noise and fury, were but a minority. The players during their sojourn in New York won a positive if not an overwhelming success, as may be judged from the following representative extracts from the dramatic reports of the time.

The Irish Players from the Abbey Theatre, Dublin, made their first appearance in the city in the Maxine Elliott Theatre on Monday evening. Their ability as actors seems to have been exaggerated, but it is possible that they may appear to better advantage in later representations. In light comedy or in the quieter passages of domestic drama they exhibited a delightful naturalness, their diction, dress, deportment, and gesture being perfectly characteristic of the peasant class which they represent. But in the more exciting episodes they reveal the need of artistic training to supplement the resources of natural intelligence. Their general freedom from self-consciousness, exaggeration, and staginess is their greatest virtue; but of perfect naturalness upon the stage, as of some other very good things, there may be too much. There is no doubt that the effect of their work could be much improved by the use of a little legitimate artifice.

The players are unsophisticated; they act with an intensity that shows how well they feel the life they portray; they speak verse with an understanding of its quality; they pass from gravity to humour—a surprising characteristic in Synge—with an adaptibility that shows art pliable in their hands. Their costumes are old and torn, green with the age of the pawnshop, grimy with the dirt of the roads. These men and women come from the rank and file of the workers, with no preparation for the stage. What they have learned they have learned in the theatre itself. Sometimes they are crude, but it is the crudity of child-like love of play. Both the Irish playwright and the Irish actor are very much like children in their naïve spirit.

We find in the acting the same sincerity of purpose and expression that we have come to look for in the plays. No devastating " star" parts break the harmony of the company, which acts as a unit intent on the just interpretation of the author. And in this school of acting, with its quiet restraint and simplicity in tragedy, its spontaneity in comedy, its fresh exuberance in farce, we attain a realism that seems reality in the absolute, if it were not for our knowledge of the study and the art that lie concealed beneath. And what a relief it is to find a company so void of self-consciousness, of posturings, and those ghastly affectations that form the scrip and scrippage of many a " star" on either side of the

Atlantic. To select any special players would seem almost an invidious task, but Maire O'Neill as Nora in *In The Shadow of the Glen,* as Pegeen Mike in *The Playboy,* and as *Deirdre,* is surely the perfect embodiment of Synge's imagination; while Miss Sara Allgood as old Maurya in *Riders to the Sea* and as Mary Doul in *The Well of the Saints,* leaves no touch of character, or pathos, or humour, undefined.

3.—*Chicago and Philadelphia.*

After the rousing reception accorded them in New York, the little Irish company went on tour, playing some of the important cities. They were well received in Chicago, in December. Returning to the east, presumably on their way to Ireland, they played in Philadelphia, which is known as the sleepy city, but which was on this occasion very wide awake. At the Adelphi Theatre much disorder greeted the appearance of *The Playboy,* and many members of a rather riotous audience were ejected. In this city prejudice and indignation went to greater lengths than heretofore; stern moralists who objected to the play had eleven of the players arrested and brought before the courts. Witnesses were examined, lawyers threshed the matter out, and the actors were held for trial. They were eventually released, the judge deciding that the charge of immorality against *The Playboy* could not be sustained.

The exhilarating American tour came to an end. The company embarked for Ireland, and arrived at Dublin in the month of March 1912, where they were given a public reception at the Royal Hibernian Academy.

BEN IDEN PAYNE.

CHAPTER X.

Winning Their Way.

1.—*Another American Tour.*

While they were away from the Abbey, Mr. Yeats had formed a second company. About this time also it had become the rage for great actors and actresses to appear for short seasons in the Music Halls (Vaudeville Houses), and offers came to the Abbey Players for such appearances, which they accepted. It was while they were fulfilling one of these engagements in Manchester, England, that Sir Oswald Stoll saw and liked their acting. Stoll is in England what Keith is in America, but on a very much smaller scale. Sir Oswald had an option on their contract for some engagements, so he exercised this option and brought them to the Coliseum, London, for five weeks. After this they returned to Dublin and played the usual Abbey season up to December, when they once more set sail for the land of the Stars and Stripes, and spent their Christmas Day on the high seas. This time they opened in Chicago for four weeks and made a wonderful hit. Here again it may be said that the people now took a saner and broader view of their plays and gave the encouragement they so richly deserved.

It was during this visit that they were invited to appear at Nôtre Dame University, in Indiana. They presented three one-act plays for the faculty and student body, a regular matinée performance. Lady Gregory and Mr. Frederick Donohey accompanied the players to Nôtre Dame. Mr. Yeats must have been with the company on this visit, as I find the following by him:—

What We Try to Do.

When the idea of giving expression on the stage to the dramatic literature of Ireland was about to be carried out in 1899 it was found that no Irish actors were to be had, so we brought an English company to Dublin and Irish plays were presented by them for a short period. This method did not, however, produce the results we hoped for; the English actors lacked the proper feeling for the Irish spirit. In 1902 there was a nearer approach to a realization of a truly national Irish Theatre, for a company of amateurs produced Irish plays in small halls in Dublin. The players received nothing, nor did they ask remuneration, since they had to gain a living by another work to carry on the work they were interested in.

The company of amateurs here referred to by Mr. Yeats was the W. G. Fay and Frank Fay Acting Company, and were it not for the existence of this little band of amateur actors at this critical moment the story of the Irish National Theatre might not have begun in the year of Our Lord 1902.

Sara Allgood, who is regarded as the genius of the Abbey and the greatest Irish actress of our time, was trained in the art of speaking by Mr. Frank J. Fay, to whom she went as a pupil for two years,

while he taught her the speaking of blank verse.
In an interview in Chicago at this time she says:
" When the Fays, the first stage managers of this
company, offered me a place among the players I
took it. I had a youngster's fascination for the
stage, and enthusiasm kept me there. The
enthusiasm of us all when this company was first
organized was really wonderful. It wasn't for
money we worked then, I can tell you it was not,
indeed, because we got between five and fifteen
shillings a week, and that only if we were lucky;
often we got nothing at all. When I was raised to
fifteen shillings a week I thought I owned the world.
At night after the play we'd chip in for a little feast,
and the boys would run out to get it, one
for tea, another for sugar, another for bread, and
so on. Many's the time I've dressed myself for my
parts in clothes I made from my mother's old
dresses, and J. M. Kerrigan used to borrow things
from his house to use as stage properties, once a
poker, another time a blanket. We had nothing of
our own, and no money to get anything with. Why
even yet I wear the old cape in *Hyacinth Halvey*
that I stole from my aunt in those days. I've never
paid her for it, but I've promised to give her five
shillings when I go back to Ireland. I studied
from life. My family have helped me a good deal,
haven't they? My mother with her old dresses, my
aunt with her shawl, and my grandmother with
herself. My granny is eighty years old, and I study
her for my old woman parts. I've watched to see
how she walks, how she leans on the table when
she gets up, how she uses her voice when she walks,

and when she is quiet. It is a grand thing to be able to study all these points at home.

" In my stage catechism the play is really and truly the thing. When producing I believe in adding nothing external, when acting I merely read as deep into the actual lines as there is depth in them to plumb. Acting is entirely a process of evolution. A part must be evolved out of the written words of the play and out of the feeling of the actor. Tricks of acting or outside aid are beneath my ideal.[1]

Finishing the Chicago engagement they next journeyed to New York, where they produced *The Playboy* to a cheering house at Wallack's Theatre. There was not a murmur of dissent. A well-known gentleman, the famous Burke Corcoran, who had been one of their bitterest enemies on their first visit in 1911, now became one of their staunchest supporters.

While on the American tour there was talk in Ireland of erecting an art gallery over the old metal toll bridge that spans the famous River Liffey at Bachelor's Walk and Aston's Quay, to exhibit the Hugh Lane collection of paintings (Hugh Lane was a nephew of Lady Gregory). The Abbey Players had generously guaranteed to give the sum of one thousand pounds toward the expenses of the proposed art gallery. The players contemplated raising the sum by playing special matinées, one of which was given at Wallack's Theatre for this purpose. Mr. Burke Corcoran was present at this special matinée. After the performance he went in front of the curtain and praised highly the plays and

1 The *Sunday Record Herald*, Feb. 4, 1912. Chicago.

the players, and compared them to the artists of the great Comédie Française in Paris. And then, to add to their glory, presented Lady Gregory with a large bouquet of flowers. The sum of eight hundred pounds was raised by these special matinées. Nothing came of the art gallery project—it was just so much talk that vanished with the mists of yesterday.

There was some discussion and much dissension about the disposal of the money which, in the end, was divided equally among the players, who had earned and no doubt deserved it.

Returning from their successful American tour they did the usual season in London and played at the Coliseum. This was in 1913, when Miss Sara Allgood left the Irish players to play in *The Great Adventure,* by Arnold Bennett, under the management of Granville Barker. *The Great Adventure* is a dramatisation of Bennett's novel " Buried Alive."

The Irish players now produced *The Bribe,* by Seumas O'Kelly, which proved to be one of the best plays of the year. Another new production was undertaken, *Duty,* by Seumas O'Brien, who had returned from America. He is the author of the great book, " The Whale and the Grasshopper."

2.—*A French Appreciation.*

In 1913, Mr. Maurice Bourgeois observed and recorded the following: —

The Abbey Theatre is now a fixture in Ireland's dramatic renaissance. Its official as well as unofficial history so far remains untold; and, indeed, it is

much too soon to attempt a record of its achievements, or form a mature judgment of its merits.
We stand too close to the picture...and a clear
vision is reserved for unborn eyes. Despite its
overwhelming vitality, as evidenced by the some
sixty Irish plays it has brought forth during these
first *eight* years of its existence, and the tremendous
impetus it has given to the Irish, Scotch, and Welsh
sections of the neo-Celtic drama, the theatre is as
yet in its infancy.[2]

Sixteen years have passed since the foregoing
article was written, and twenty-five since the opening of the Abbey, during which time its directors,
dramatists, plays, and actors have gained world-
wide recognition. Poor, despised, down-trodden
Ireland in these years has arisen from her long
slumber, and called to her children to show the
world that within the green isle there were young
men and women within whose very being burned the
fires of genius, which lay but smouldering, until the
light of opportunity should set them ablaze in their
own fair land.

For the long hidden and God-given gifts of these
men and women of talent a theatre was found in
which they could show to the world the treasures
that lay hid within their being. Ireland in the past
was forced to see her sons depart to foreign lands,
where an outlet could be found for their talent, but
in the year 1904 Ireland's first subsidized theatre
flung open its doors with a Céad Míle Fáilte to the
genius of her country.

A quick response came forth; actors and authors

2 *Mr. John Millington Synge and the Irish Theatre.* By
Maurice Bourgeois, p. 127—128.

crowded in from all over the country with results that have astounded the world. Aubrey de Vere said: "Whatever develops the genius of Ireland must in the most effectual way benefit her, and in Ireland's genius I have long been a strong believer."

3.—*America Once More.*

The year 1914 saw a return visit to America, opening in Chicago, then across to Toronto in Canada. *The Playboy* was played at the Princess Theatre in the latter city and caused a mild kind of trouble. This incident is well worth recording, more on account of the amusing situation than for the disturbance. A committee was formed to inquire into the merits or demerits of *The Playboy,* under the direction of one Tom Flanagan, trainer of Jack Johnson, the negro fighter, and former champion boxer of the world. The committee did not understand a thing about the play, but *The Playboy*'s reputation had become world-wide, and the citizens of Toronto, not to be outdone by the citizens of any other part of the globe, thought it was within their rights to give *The Playboy* the "once-over."[3] Mr Arthur Sinclair happened to meet the renowned Flanagan and asked him what he thought of the play. Tom gave a broad grin and replied, "Begob I think he's the real playboy." However, the renowned Mr. Sydney Morgan was asked to explain to the Committee the plot of *The Playboy.* Sydney loves to talk, is very proficient

[3] An American slang expression for judging a person or thing.

and prolific, and by the time he was through with the Toronto committee they were ready to canonize the poor *Playboy*. Objections and discussions again took place when *Blanco Posnet* was billed. The players were advised to withdraw it and substitute something else, which they did.

From Toronto they jumped to Boston, but for one matinée only, as they were booked to sail on the "Carmania." There was some talk of the company leaving on the "Empress of Ireland," but circumstances arose which made it impossible. The "Empress of Ireland" left the harbour at Boston and carried among its passengers the famous London actress, Miss Mabel Hackney and her husband, Mr. Laurence Irving, son of Sir Henry Irving, who were drowned when the ship was lost at sea.

The original booking on the old reliable "Carmania" stood, and on this ship they sailed for Liverpool, England. Miss Sara Allgood rejoined the company on their arrival and resumed her old parts. This year, made memorable by the commencement of the World War, was one full of activity with appearances in Dublin and London. Again Miss Allgood left the company to play Nannie in *The Little Minister,* by J. M. Barrie, under the Charles Frohman management. At the conclusion of this engagement she returned to the Abbey company and crossed to London with them to play at the Little Theatre, just off the Strand, also at the Coliseum in *Duty,* and a play of Lady Gregory's. On the boat crossing to London they had as passengers the survivors of the ill-fated "Lusitania."

Mr. George Bernard Shaw wrote *O'Flaherty, V.C.* for the Abbey, to be produced in 1915. Arthur Sinclair was to play the lead, in fact the part was written for him by Shaw. The military in Ireland at that time advised the directors of the Abbey that they would close the theatre if any trouble took place at the presentation of *O'Flaherty, V.C.*, so it was decided to postpone the production indefinitely. Almost the whole of the year 1915 was spent playing the Music Halls or Vaudeville Houses.

CHAPTER XI.

THE ST. JOHN ERVINE EPISODE AT THE ABBEY.

1.—*A Want of Tact.*

AT the conclusion of this tour in the month of November, Mr. St. John Ervine became manager of the Abbey Theatre and players. Whether the directors had given him the power denied to Mr. W. G. Fay it is impossible to say. However, Mr. Ervine was anxious to make good and show his ability as producer and writer, and lost no time in producing his own play, *John Ferguson.* In the cast appeared his wife, Miss Norah Close, who played the leading lady's part. She appeared also in a few other plays, e.g., *In the Shadow of the Glen* and *The Bribe.*

Miss Close did not seem to make much of an impression in her parts, and wisely withdrew from the stage as an actress. Miss Sara Allgood left the Abbey company at this time to play Peg in *Peg o' My Heart,* by Hartley Manners. She toured England with this play and went with it to Australia, where she remained for some few years.

This brought them into the year 1916, when they went over to Liverpool and played a two-weeks' engagement, afterwards returning to Dublin in Easter week, for an eight weeks' run at the Abbey.

It was on this very Easter Monday the Irish Rebellion broke out under the leadership of Padraic Pearse. This turned the whole country topsy-turvy for a time, and while the fighting went on it was impossible to open the doors of the theatre to present any plays.

But in the month of May the theatre was opened and some plays were presented. Then the company made a trip to Limerick to play one week at the Theatre Royal. Mr. Ervine had for some time been giving trouble to the company, and it was here in Limerick that it reached the boiling point.

The players were rehearsing *The Playboy* by way of revival for the Abbey. They had a rule among themselves—it was an unwritten one, but, nevertheless, it had stood for years—to the effect that if the company was not playing they rehearsed twice each day; if playing at night, they rehearsed once; if playing a matinée they did not rehearse at all. Mr. Ervine, in a very imperious manner, called a rehearsal out of time; the tone and the command were naturally resented by the players. If he had asked as a gentleman and in a friendly way, the players would willingly have acceded to his request. But his request happened to be a haughty and imperious command, so under the circumstances existing at that time the pot boiled over. Mr. Ervine, in other words, tried to make a command of a rule, and so here the trouble reached its climax. The hour, 3 p.m., appointed by Mr. Ervine for the extra rehearsal arrived, but it did not bring the players, except Arthur Sinclair, who went to the theatre as spokesman and told Mr. Ervine that the players would not come, that they refused to be dictated to, and that they regarded him in the light of a paid servant. This abruptly closed the interview. At the theatre that night Mr. Ervine asked the players why they did not turn up for the rehearsal, and as none of the players chose to answer, the matter remained thus. The company returned to Dublin to play *The Playboy,* but on Saturday night Mr. Ervine left letters for the entire company informing the players that their contracts were terminated; that they could go, and that all engagements booked in England were cancelled. The following Monday the players met in the green room of the Abbey and discussed the situation. They decided to wire to Lady Gregory to learn if Mr. Ervine had power to dismiss the company. They waited for three hours, but Lady Gregory failed to reply within that time. (She did reply by letter, which arrived the following day and entirely too late).

The players knew the people would come and expect to see *The Playboy* that evening, as it was billed; so to get over the difficulty they had slips printed and handed to those who were waiting outside the theatre. While the bills were being distributed some of the people went in and others continued to follow. The following is the exact wording on the printed slips: —

To the Patrons of the Abbey Theatre.

The Players regret to disappoint their public this week, as they cannot appear under the present manager, Mr. St. John Ervine; full particulars will appear in the Press.

One of the boys who was distributing the bills presented a copy to Mr. Ervine on his arrival. This was the first intimation he had of what was in the air. He immediately went into the theatre, and, not finding the players there, he went on the stage and spoke to the few people present, offering some kind of apology and saying there would be no performance that evening. The affair raised a great discussion in the papers, theatrically and otherwise. On Tuesday morning Mr. Ervine went to the theatre as usual and meeting the players there he tried to become friendly, but they told him they were through, and positively refused to play, at the same time telling Mr. Ervine that instead of his dismissing them they now dismissed him.

2.—*The Irish Players.*

The exact date of the culmination of the dispute between the players and Mr. Ervine was May 29, 1916, and this was Mr. Arthur Sinclair's last day at the Abbey as an actor. He returned the following day to remove some of his property. Previous to this row Mr. Sinclair had tendered his resignation to Mr. Ervine, saying that he would not continue beyond the end of the season.

After Mr. Sinclair and the other players had departed from their beloved Abbey Theatre, where they had worked so hard and become so famous, they went over to the Central Hotel in George's and Exchequer Streets and rented a large room there. The directors and St. John Ervine had an idea that the company would crawl back, but in this they made the mistake of their lives. Mr. Yeats, a few days after the split, rang up the Central Hotel and asked to speak to Miss Cathleen Drago, and spoke to her about a Miss Helen Moloney, who had played at the Abbey; this was by way of breaking the ice. Mr. Yeats then asked if Miss Drago had anything to say to him, to which she replied that she had not and then hung up the receiver.

Sinclair and the players discussed the situation over and over. Finally they decided on forming a company of their own, and within a space of two weeks The Irish Players, headed by Mr. Arthur Sinclair, were on the road playing an engagement at Belfast.

On the opening night at the Grand Opera House, Mr. Sinclair and Mr. McCann, the manager of the house, were served with legal papers to the effect that the directors of the Abbey Theatre would apply for an injunction to restrain them from producing the Abbey Theatre plays, but the matter was dropped.

Mr. William Boyle and most of the other playwrights offered Mr. Sinclair their plays, and very many letters were received by him conveying congratulations on the break with Mr. Ervine. Mr. W. W. Kelley, of *A Royal Divorce* fame, brought the new company of the Sinclair Irish Players over to the Shakespeare Theatre, Liverpool, for an engagement, and they did wonderful business there.

The agent who formally booked them for the Music Halls (Vaudevile Houses) now sought them out and gave them back the engagements and contracts which Mr. Ervine had cancelled. A great tour was made through England, and while it was in progress Mr. Ervine's fate was hanging in the balance at the Abbey. However, the directors did not let him " hang" for long; they kindly requested him to resign, which he finally did. So ended the St. John Ervine reign of terror.

CHAPTER XII.

CHANGES OF MANAGEMENT.

1.—*Keogh and O'Donovan.*

HE was succeeded by Augustus J. Keogh, the great Shavian producer, who remained at the Abbey only a very short time; but while there he produced Shaw's *Man and Superman, The Doctor's Dilemma,* and *The Inca of Perusalem.* The Abbey audiences have a partiality for Shavian drama, and seem to relish very much the Shavian irony in the dialogue. Shaw's plays can attract attention almost anywhere, and are so much good copy for the critics. Mr. Keogh, the new manager, and Mr. William Boyle, the author of many Abbey plays, made overtures to Mr. Sinclair about returning to the Abbey. In fact, an article appeared in the Dublin " Evening Herald" to the effect that the entire company was returning, but the whole thing was a fabrication. One could read, who cared to read, that it was just a ruse or a hint to the players that they would be welcomed with open arms by the directors if they cared to return. The Sinclair Irish Players had at this time more engagements than they could fulfil, and were working very happily together, with never a thought of returning to resume work under the Abbey management.

T. C. MURRAY.

In the spring of 1917, Mr. Augustus Keogh gave up his position as manager of the Abbey to start as a producer for himself. He was succeeded by Mr. Fred O'Donovan, who managed, acted, and produced. He held the position up to April 1919, and under his direction were produced *The Grabber,* by E. F. Barrett; *A Little Bit of Youth,* by C. Callister; *Sable and Gold,* by Maurice Dalton; *When Love Came Over the Hills,* by W. R. Fearon and Roy Nesbitt; *Hanrahan's Oath* and *The Dragon,* by Lady Gregory; *Aliens,* by Rose McKenna; *Spring,* by T. C. Murray; *The Lost Leader,* by Lennox Robinson, and many other plays.

2.—*Robinson and Dolan.*

Mr. Lennox Robinson took over the reins as soon as Mr. O'Donovan resigned, and carried on up to the year 1921 when he became a director and was succeeded by that capable actor, Mr. Michael Dolan, who was entrusted with the management.

The reason of this change was that some of the players went to America to play in *The White-headed Boy,* by Lennox Robinson—a play which did not meet with the approval of the New York audiences, and which turned out to be a hopeless failure, though it had a run of nine months in 1920 at the Ambassador's Theatre in London.

The year 1921 was a remarkable one in many instances, several fine plays being produced, including *Bedmates,* by Mr. George Shiels, which proved to be one of the cleverest and funniest of pieces, and which scored an overwhelming success. Another play of his, *Insurance Money,* was produced this year. The most remarkable feature of Mr. Shiels's work is that it is bubbling over with wit and humour. He never wrote a play till he became a cripple. The sad thing about this young author is that he can never see any of his plays at the Abbey.

A very interesting event happened this season, Mr. Frank Fay returned to the Abbey to play his old part in *The King's Threshold,* by W. B. Yeats. New actors occupy the boards to-day, and there is no dearth of merit. But as long as the Abbey Theatre exists the names of Frank Fay and W. G. Fay will be recalled in connection with it.

Another striking event was the action taken by the Sinn Féiners. In March of this year the Abbey Players were rehearsing *The Revolutionist,* by Terence MacSwiney, when the stage was rushed by the Sinn Féin men to prohibit anyone photographing any situations of the play, and objecting to anyone making capital of the play, saying that MacSwiney was guilty of propaganda against Sinn Féin. The author of *The Revolutionist* became world-famous while undergoing a hunger-strike, from the effects of which he died in an English prison.

The Abbey directors now began to consider the advisability of opening a School of Acting from which they could draw recruits to fill the ranks of those who might leave to seek fame and glory in other companies or countries. The theatre building extends some distance down Abbey Street, and within its walls was a large library which was remodelled into a little theatre by Mr. Michael Scott, an actor at the Abbey, and also an architect in the firm of Jones and Kelly, South Frederick Street, Dublin. It is a complete theatre in itself, has its own box-office, and seats one hundred and fifteen. The stage is about two-and-a-half feet in height from the floor, two steps leading to the stage, and running right across the front. There are no foot-lights, but head- or fly-lights and side-lights, which are concealed from the audience. The stage equipment and dressing room accommodation are perfect.

The little theatre may be let out to societies for the production of their plays. Any new writer can rent the theatre and produce his work, and every attention will be given his play by critics as if produced in the Abbey Theatre itself. The training of the pupil consists in voice production and naturalistic acting; the number of pupils is limited, this being necessary as there are more applicants than could possibly be handled with care and attention. Previous to this the small parts in the Abbey plays were taken by raw amateurs, but now such parts are capably filled by the Little Theatre recruits. Mr. Michael Dolan is the director of the new School of Acting, and it could not be in better or more capable hands. He is a wonderful producer, and gave every proof of his ability along these lines while acting as manager of the Abbey. One very notable success from the School of Acting was made by Miss Eileen Crowe, who is now the Abbey's leading lady. No other actress has achieved such distinction at the theatre since the days of Miss Sara Allgood.

The Abbey company went to England in 1922 and played an engagement at the Winter Garden, New Brighton. The venture was a success artistically, but an absolute failure financially, owing to a tremendous heat wave which interfered sadly with every kind of business. Work was again resumed at the Abbey with Sara Allgood, its most distinguished actress who has written her name largely on the theatrical scroll of fame. It is very significant to note that after the Black-and-Tan war business at the theatre assumed much larger proportions, and this even in the face of disasters and the death of Arthur Griffith, the father of Sinn Féin and the President of the Provisional Government; also the killing of Michael Collins, Commanding-General of the Free State army.

A new play, *Paul Twyning,* by George Shiels, was produced this year—a light comedy which attracted much favourable notice. Another, *Ann Kavanagh,* by Dorothy McArdle met with some favour. In this year also *The Young Man from Rathmines* and *A Lepraucaun in the Tenement,* both by M. M. Brennan, were produced with success. *The Moral Law,* by R. J. Ray, was also shown.

In October of the year 1922, the night before the execution of Erskine Childers, the audience could not leave the theatre until after midnight owing to the fact that the Free Staters and Republicans were firing and sniping outside the theatre. They were playing *The Eloquent Dempsey* in the Abbey. During the third act the noise outside was simply terrible. There was a guard on the roof during the playing of the piece; later on, however, the noise

subsided; then in the early hours of the morning
the actors and audience were able to leave the
theatre for their homes.

This took them over Christmas up to the great
sensation of the new year 1923—*The Shadow of a
Gunman,* by Seán O'Casey.

About the month of April of the same year the
fighting and shooting in and around Dublin became
very severe, nevertheless the Abbey kept its doors
open until the summer, when the ambushes made
it dangerous to go abroad during the night. *The
Gunman* shared the bill with *Crabbed Youth and
Age,* by Lennox Robinson, which continued to be a
great favourite with Dublin audiences. The O'Casey
and Robinson plays made frequent appearances
during the year, and on every occasion were hailed
with delight.

It was in this year, 1923, that the Republicans
objected to the Dublin theatres being kept open.
Mr. Ruttledge, the Acting-President of the Republican movement in Ireland, commanded all places
of amusement to be closed down. But the Abbey
Theatre opened as usual and played in spite of him.
On St. Patrick's night, March 17, 1923, the Abbey
actors played W. B. Yeats's *Shadowy Waters* under
the protection of an armed guard from the National
Free State Army for one week, and continued their
repertoire under a detachment of detectives for
three months. This particular St. Patrick's Day is
notable by the fact that Battling Siki and Mike
McTigue did battle for the light-heavyweight
championship of the world under a guard of
soldiers at the La Scala Theatre Picture House, off

O'Connell Street, Dublin. After the fight the back portion of the theatre was blown out by a bomb.

Brinsley MacNamara's play, *The Glorious Uncertainty,* was produced this year. It proved to be a splendid play dealing with horse-racing in the midlands of Ireland. It was greeted with much approval, in fact had a glorious reception. MacNamara's play had the able assistance of Sara Allgood, Barry Fitzgerald, and Michael Dolan, three players of renown, to make it a success, and if the play itself had any merit it could not possibly fail in such capable hands. Mr. Barry Fitzgerald is regarded to-day as one of the greatest players that have trod the boards of the Abbey stage in its twenty-five years of existence.

CHAPTER XIII.

SENSATIONS AND SUCCESSES.

1.—A Schoolmaster Genius.

THE season of 1924 proved to be one of sensations and successes. The first sensation was the appearance of Mr. Lennox Robinson as an actor in the title-rôle of Pirandello's *Henry IV*. Mr. Robinson created quite a sensation by his wonderful acting in the part of the mock King Henry IV. The audience were surprised and amazed by the brilliancy of his truly marvellous performance. Up to this time he was thought of only as a writer and producer, but he showed that he is capable of other accomplishments.

The second sensation was the production of Seán O'Casey's marvellous play *Juno and the Paycock*, in April 1924, with the celebrated Sara Allgood in the rôle of Juno, which turned out to be one of the greatest successes of her brilliant career.

In this year, 1924, *Autumn Fire*, by T. C. Murray, was produced at the Abbey but did not receive much recognition. But on its presentation in London it met with a brilliant and instantaneous success. It was speedily recognized as a great play, and its author was hailed as the schoolmaster genius. His own home town awoke to the fact that another great playwright was born amongst them. Crowds besieged the Abbey to see the play which previously they had neglected. It was in *Autumn Fire* that Mr. Michael Dolan gave the most wonderful performance of his career; in fact, his characterization of Owen Keegan was one of the outstanding studies of the year. Sara Allgood, as the spinster sister added much to her reputation. *Autumn Fire* was presented in New York at the Klaw Theatre in 1926 by J. L. Shine with a supposedly all-Irish cast. Miss Una O'Connor, who was trained at the Abbey, was imported from London to play the leading lady's part. With the exception of Miss O'Connor, I do not think any of the other players ever saw Ireland except on the map or read about it in history. Mr. Murray's beautiful play was done to death by the forced brogue of the New Yorkers, and withdrawn after a few performances.

The busy and artistic Lennox Robinson presented for the admiration of the Abbey patrons a well-written and well-staged play, *Never the Time and the Place.* Any play from the pen of Mr. Robinson commands attention, and this play of his proved no exception to the rule. Mr. Robinson is not only a favourite with the Abbey patrons, but also a great favourite with the players.

The name of Lady Gregory, that grand old lady, and the fairy godmother of the Abbey, once again came into prominence with a new play entitled *The Story Brought by Brigit.* This play is supposed to be the account of a story brought to Ireland by Saint Brigid, and about the saint having seen Christ.

Mr. F. J. McCormick played the part of Pontius Pilate, and an unknown Trinity College student, Mr. Lyle Donnahy, a golden-haired, clean-shaven, splendid-looking boy played the symbol of Our Lord very effectively. In the play this character was referred to as " He." Miss Sara Allgood took part in the play; but off stage she sang the lamentations, and the beauty of her voice will not soon be forgotten; the sad and plaintive notes were sung by her with much effect, which lent an atmosphere of sadness and beauty to the play and made it most impressive.

The production reflected the greatest credit on all concerned, but such presentations will never become very popular with Irish audiences. We Irish are of a spiritual race and no matter how far we fall short of what we should be in our lives, we hold God and all His things sacred, in such reverence, awe, and wonder that it seems almost profanity to us to see anyone attempt the portrayal of sacred personages. This is one of the main reasons of the play's failure to attract much attention.

Early in 1925 another remarkable play had its première in the Abbey, *Professor Tim,* by George Shiels, and it was a tremendous success. In this play Mr. F. J. McCormick made one of the greatest hits of his artistic career. I had the pleasure of seeing his superb portrayal in the character of the Professor, and to my mind, after nearly forty years of theatre-going and playing, it was one of the best drawn character performances I ever remember to have seen. Another very notable revival in this year was *Maurice Harte,* by T. C. Murray, in which Mr.

McCormick again scored a signal triumph. There seems to be no limit to the talents of this truly great actor.

The Abbey Players have a warm spot in their hearts for the lovable George Bernard Shaw, with all his faults—and they are many to those who do not know him intimately. But to those who have that privilege he is the kindest, jolliest, and gentlest old man that one could imagine. George Bernard Shaw looks at the world through the eyes of a mischievous child, who loves to tease and contradict for the sake of argument, and who does not believe or intend others to believe half of what he writes or says. In the language of America, Shaw is a great "kidder."

Fannie's First Play, written by him, was staged at the Abbey and met with the usual Shaw success. Also *The Big House,* by Lennox Robinson, met with acclamations of approval. The play deals with a class of people quite the opposite to the O'Casey characters of slum life. Another play of Robinson's appeared the same year entitled *The White Blackbird;* Lady Gregory, the tireless, staged a translation from the Russian drama, *The Proposal,* by the great Russian author, Tchekoff, and yet another, *The Would-be Gentleman,* by Molière.

2.—*The Abbey Comes of Age.*

On the 27th December, 1925, Ireland's representative theatre, the Abbey, celebrated its twenty-first birthday. Mr. Yeats, who brought it into being, was present on this memorable day, as no doubt he was on the first night of its opening, December 27, 1904. How proud he must have been on both occasions! The first night the Abbey opened its doors to the public and the curtain was drawn to reveal its first play, *On Baile's Strand,* written by himself, he saw the realization of his dreams come true; and on the second occasion, twenty-one years later, he undoubtedly looked back on those years of accomplishment, during which time two hundred and sixteen plays have been produced, the work of eighty-six authors. Lady Gregory was too ill to be present on the opening night twenty-one years before, but she was present with Mr. Yeats on this anniversary night. On this night she must have felt a twinge of the pride and joy that comes to every conqueror in the hour of success—and Lady Gregory must be regarded as a conqueror, for has she not carried her little theatre through twenty-one years of struggle and strife, when friends and helpers turned against her and left her almost stranded, when seemingly insurmountable obstacles had barred her way and tried to hold her back? Through her unflagging energy, zeal, and ability as a dramatic writer she had kept the little Abbey Theatre steadily marching onward, until it has reached the highest pinnacle of fame as the leading and most distinguished little theatre in the world. Lady Gregory never faltered on the way or even looked back, but kept plodding on and on towards the goal that at times looked far away. " I am going on as long as life is left in me "—this was her motto —nil desperandum. She never despaired through those long weary years. Just a few days ago she wrote to me as follows:—" The chief thing of late has been the granting of a subsidy of £800, and now £1,000 to us by the Government of the Irish Free State. We are proud of this, especially as England has not yet an endowed theatre." It is a great, just, and fitting tribute to Lady Gregory and W. B. Yeats that their work should be recognized by the government of Saorstát Eireann with such a substantial subsidy. Under the guiding hands and watchful eyes, the wise direction and clever management of Lady Gregory and W. B. Yeats, the Abbey Theatre has become one of the most interesting phenomena in the whole sphere of dramatic art. It stands alone and beyond all other little theatres. As Max Beerbohm tersely puts it, " It is the only oasis amidst the sandy desert of the theatrical world generally." In a word, it is the world's Little Theatre *par excellence*.

CHAPTER XIV.

SEAN O'CASEY.

1.—*The Shadow of a Gunman.*

IT will be convenient at this point to deal in some detail with Seán O'Casey's contributions to the Abbey Repertoire. Up to the writing of *The Shadow of a Gunman,* of whose production in 1923 mention has been already made, O'Casey was a Dublin labourer and a member of the Labour Union with headquarters at Liberty Hall. The labourers wanted to get up a concert for Christmas, and O'Casey said he would write them a play, which he did with the significant title *On the Run.* The play was such a success that he was encouraged to send it to the directors of the Abbey Theatre for production. The directors, captivated by its power and novel construction, informed him that if he changed the name they would accept it for production. He was so excited and elated over the Abbey directors' promise that he spent much of his time trying to think out a suitable name. One night he was trying to work by the faint light of a candle, and being tired, he fell into a light sleep, in which he had some kind of a confused dream. Waking out of this sleep he thought he heard someone moving in his room. The candle light was flickering and casting weird shadows on the walls, some of which brought to his mind the shadowy figures of gunmen who were then prowling the streets of Dublin. Like a flash the name came to him for his play—*The Shadow of a Gunman*—so goes the tale of the O'Casey play.

This was O'Casey's introduction to Irish playgoers. *The Shadow of a Gunman* was an instantaneous success, and brought its author into the light as a dramatic genius and a worthy successor of J. M. Synge. It was, however, but an earnest of what was to come.

2.—*Juno and the Paycock.*

Juno and the Paycock, produced in April of the following year, was without doubt the greatest and most astounding success in the history of the Abbey Theatre. The audience went wild with delight and kept applauding and cheering and calling for the author. But O'Casey would not appear until Lennox Robinson actually carried him from the stalls where he was crouching and hiding in a seat. The audience could not restrain themselves, a crowd rushed round to the stage door and forced their way in to reach O'Casey in order to congratulate him. *Juno* was billed for one week, which is the usual way of all plays, but all rules, regulations, and traditions were broken for this once, and *Juno* was allowed to hold the stage for a run of two weeks. *Juno and the Paycock* made O'Casey famous, and brought the little Abbey Theatre once again into the spotlight of the world. The leading parts were played by Sara Allgood as Juno, Barry Fitzgerald as Captain Jack Boyle, and the renowned F. J. McCormick as Joxer Daly. To one who has neither read O'Casey's book nor seen his play, the following synopsis will serve some purpose.

Mrs. Boyle, the Juno of the play, is replying to her lout of a husband's suggestion that they and their cronies, enjoying whiskey and song in a Dublin tenement, needn't mind the tragedies of war, ambush, and reprisal going on all about them.

" I'd like to know," she says, " how a body's not to mind these things; look at the way they're after leavin' the people in this very house. Hasn't the whole house, nearly, been massacreed? There's young Mrs. Dougherty's husband with his leg off; Mrs. Travers that had her son blew up be a mine in Inchegeela; Mrs. Mannin' that lost wan of her sons in an ambush a few weeks ago, an' now, poor Mrs. Tancred's only child gone west with his body made a collandher of. Sure, if it's not our business, I don't know whose business it is." And so here is the drama of the dark days, the dark deeds and sufferings of Ireland from 1916 to 1923, from the standpoint of the Dublin tenement-dwellers, whose business it all very much was. Seldom has an epoch been put so promptly on the stage. As the years recede, the story of the fight for liberty, and the even grimmer story of the ghastly civil war, will yield themes to other dramatists who, rightly enough, will dress them forth in the high heroic mood. But it is probably that the clammy hands of sentimentality will never fashion a sugary melo-drama in the old romantic vein out of the incidents of these years; the merciless, mordant, irrefutable realism of Seán O'Casey has rendered that impossible, and the gale of his sardonic irony blows fiercely enough to warn all painted and hollow puppets off the stage. It is no wonder this play instantly brought Dublin to the feet of a new and unknown dramatist. It is more than a mirror held up to nature. It is nature itself—human nature, so living and quick that Dublin must have forgotten proscenium and footlights as it watched; while only those unfortunate enough never to have known simple Irish folk, and so limited in experience as never to have moved among tenement-dwellers in the dank gloom of poverty, can fail to feel, as they read the mere printed words, that they are actually living in the two squalid rooms of the Boyles with the swaggering Paycock, the patient, tragic Juno, the aspiring, helmless Mary, the haunted Johnny, and the fawning, drunken, thieving Joxer. It is Sean O'Casey's distinction as a dramatist that he has successfully dared to move to his awful climax of tragedy through scenes of roaring farce. For the farce is as true as the tragedy. It would have been easy to develop this theme in an Ibsenish atmosphere of sombre solemnity, but the truth of life would have gone out of it. The heroisms and the crimes and the terrors of that awful birth from which present-day Ireland has come, were very largely the doing of just such boys as Johnny—daring, crude, finally bewildered and stricken down—who came from just such homes, with sodden, drunken, lazy fathers, like Jack Boyle, holding all down to a level of whiskey-and-porter-soaked poverty.

SEAN O'CASEY.

Jack Boyle, the Paycock, is a tremendous figure. In his youth doubtless a sturdy worker, under the crushing weight of labour and years he has saturated himself with drink till all he desires is the long somnolence of loafing in a " snug," spending his last " make" with a wily parasite who flatters him and insults him alternately. A vast pagan figure of a man, lying about his adventures at sea; falling victim to pains in his legs whenever a job threatens; scorning the Church and deriding the clergy one day and defending them the next; swaggering in gaudy, vulgar exuberance when he thinks he is coming into an inheritance; and at last finding forgetfulness of the dishonour of his daughter, the murder of his son, and the martyrdom of his wife in a drunken stupor on the bare floor of the room from which the instalment-house men have removed the last stick of furniture. Joxer Daly, too, with his ever-ready proverb, his snatches of poetry, his flattery and lies and petty thefts, is a masterly bit out of life.

Under their drunken, unheeding eyes their women suffer, and the savageries of reprisal let loose on Ireland reduce the soldier son to a cowering wretch shrieking for pity as he is dragged forth to death. The ancient faith of Ireland flickers among these people as dimly as the little lights before the statues of the Virgin and Saint Anthony that hang on their walls; only in the crushed heart of Mrs. Boyle it remains unquenched; and with a verbal unorthodoxy that puts a shining truth blunderingly, but sublimely, she sums it all up in these terrible words: " Ah, what can God do agen the stupidity o' men!"

3.—*The Plough and the Stars.*

The year 1926 saw the production of what is now very generally considered O'Casey's masterpiece —*The Plough and the Stars.* This play was attended with turmoil from the very outset. To begin with it gave rise to much dissatisfaction and dissension among the players. Miss Eileen Crowe positively refused to play the part of Rosie Redmond, the prostitute, which is now considered one of the greatest parts in the piece. It is now being played in America with the Irish Players with Miss Cathleen Drago in the part making the success of her career. After much discussion and wrangling the part was given to Miss Ria Mooney. The night of *The Plough's* production the house was completely sold out. The literati of Ireland were there, including Liam O'Flaherty, A.E., Yeats, Walter Starkie, and many others. The première passed off peacefully, but from the second night a turmoil was brewing. O'Casey, full of excitement and anxiety, kept flitting here and there among the audience, waiting and watching for the slightest sign of dissent, disapproval, or trouble, his eyes shining with the suppressed emotions stirring within him. On Thursday night, just at the opening of the second act when Rosie Redmond, the prostitute, made her entrance, the pent-up feelings of the audience, which consisted mostly of those in favour of the Republican element, burst forth into a terrific disturbance.

Men and women rushed in a frenzied manner towards the stage and attempted to drag the actors down to the main floor. One man did succeed in getting on to the stage and started to strike the actors. But Barry Fitzgerald, who was playing Fluter Good, gave him all the fight he wanted and more than he craved with a little over for good measure. Barry set himself for one good blow, which he landed fairly and squarely under the would-be fighter's chin and sent him flying into the stalls. In the midst of the terrible din Mr. Yeats had the curtain dropped, went in front of it, and tried to speak. But it was impossible to hear what he did say beyond these few words: "All great men who have tried to do anything for art at the Abbey have met with the same reception; J. M. Synge and others, and now Seán O'Casey."

This closed the riot inside, so the audience departed to renew hostilities again whenever the opportunity offered. The following night, Friday, the theatre was crowded, but the audience were kept well under control by a detachment from the new Free State Government. Later on, when *The Plough* was to be produced, three men went to the home of Mr. Barry Fitzgerald, some think to kidnap him, but fortunately he was away, and the reason of their call still remains a mystery.

I was on a visit to Ireland about this time, and went to the Abbey Theatre to see the now famous *Plough*. The house was sold out with the exception of a few seats in the pit or stalls. I called to the stage door and asked for Mr. Michael Dolan. He was preparing in his dressing-room, but very kindly sent one of the attendants to conduct myself and Mr. William O'Brien, my nephew, to an unreserved seat before the doors opened to admit the waiting audience outside. This was my first visit to the Abbey Theatre since I had played there under the management of J. B. Carrickford and Madame Louise Grafton.

I was amazed and pleased at the transformation that had taken place in those twenty-three years. As I sat enchanted and musing the doors were opened and in a very short time the little theatre was filled and the play began. The first act passed off peacefully, but the moment Miss Ria Mooney appeared in the character of Rosie Redmond hissing could be heard from all over the house, and in a few moments a most terrible odour arose from asafoetida bombs which had been dropped by some of the dissenters in the audience. Smoking, a taboo in the theatre, began, for when the asafoetida started to waft its pestiferous perfume, matches were struck, and almost everyone began smoking cigarettes. A lady sitting nearby begged, for heaven's sake, for a cigarette. I was sorry not to be able to oblige her, but my nephew came to the rescue. The Free State detectives were active through the house and were kept busy searching for bombs, which they at times found, but not the persons who dropped them.

Around me in all directions sat young men and ladies of the student type, but each wore a look of childish innocence that would do credit to a saint with a halo in a stained glass window. To counteract the terrible odour some attendants sprayed perfume around the theatre. I thoroughly enjoyed the performance both off and on the stage.

The novelty of sitting in a theatre in which I had played for the first time twenty-three years ago, and of listening to actors who neither spoke nor acted as ordinary players do, was most agreeable and enjoyable. I thought *The Plough and the Stars* very interesting. It is a vivid and realistic drama of the Revolution of 1916. O'Casey knows Dublin, also the virtues and faults of the people who live in its tenement houses. The scenes of the play are laid in the few rooms that make up the Clitheroe home, a public house, a street outside the Clitheroe tenement, and a room within the same house. Clitheroe is a commandant in the Citizen Army, and is drawn into the vortex of civil warfare despite the violent protestations of his young wife. The atmosphere of the Revolution, including the sound of street battles and the burning of Dublin is off-stage with the exception that one of the speakers of the insurgency is seen and heard through the window of the public house, haranguing the citizens to arms.

While the men argue and drink the women do the worrying, feel the suffering, and carry the burdens of life, and either moan for their dead or are gathered in by the grim reaper, Death. The drama is a study in Irish character with all its inconsistencies, with farce merging into comedy, comedy into drama, love and hate running rampant in a whimsical topsy-turvy. But through it all there is broad strong characterization that only one who has loved and suffered among this people could have had the talent to sketch with such sharp outlines.

CHAPTER XV.

AN ANCIENT AND SOME MODERNS.

1.—*Sophocles in Dublin.*

DECEMBER of 1926 saw W. B. Yeats's version of Sophocles' "Œdipus Tyrannus" under the title of *Œdipus the King,* produced at the Abbey to an audience that packed every available space in the house. This production will stand out as one of his greatest achievements. The plot follows the original drama closely. Here again Mr. F. J. McCormick showed that he is a master of his craft. The working out of the King's own destruction mid a tangle of hope and fear, and the heartbreaking parting from his children, left a deep and lasting impression. This play makes a notable addition to the Abbey repertory and adds lustre to W. B. Yeats's already great name. The following criticisms by Mr. J. J. Hayes deserve a place in this humble history of the Abbey:—

Nowadays one associates Greek drama with the classroom or with specially arranged performances for the edification of the intellectuals. One does not expect to see an audience, drawn from all ranks of life, crowding a theatre beyond its capacity, and becoming awed into spellbound, breathless attention by a tragedy of Sophocles. Yet that is exactly what happened at the Abbey Theatre on the evening of

December 7, when W. B. Yeats's translation of
Œdipus the King was presented for the first time
by the Abbey players. It was completely a night of
unlooked for revelations, which embraced the play,
translator, players, and audience alike.

It was an event unparalleled in the history
of the Abbey, and when the chorus, standing before
the closed curtain, spoke the concluding line,
" Call no man happy while he lives," there followed
a scene of enthusiasm surpassing all similar scenes
with which the career of the theatre is dotted. It
was a spontaneous tribute, such as almost beggared
belief. To begin with, Mr. Yeats discarded the
methods of all other translators and, instead of
verse, he clothed the play in a prose which suited
the players and was equally facile as far as the
audience was concerned. This is not to say that the
version has been brought down to the level of
modern stage language. On the contrary, the
author has employed the literary touch, but in such
a way that it cannot be described as " caviare to the
general," and he never fails to give relief just at the
right moment.

Every character in the tragedy, from the mighty
figure of Œdipus down to the priest, who has only
a few lines in the opening scene, is human, while
yet preserving the lofty dignity inseparable from
the Greeks of ancient history. The lines of the
chorus alone are in verse, but here again the author
has departed from precedent. Instead of one chorus
there are eight, who, placed in front of and below
the level of the stage, on either side of steps leading
from the auditorium to the stage, represent the
Theban populace. Set to a plain chant, the lines
are divided among the eight and are rendered in
solo fashion by the different members, while the
ensemble, chanting together occasionally, convey
the impression of the comments of a crowd. This
method was extremely effective, and it held the
attention when a single chorus would have become
monotonous and tedious. In the actual drama itself

as acted on the stage there is not a moment in which the interest drops. Even the last long speech of Œdipus was not only acceptable, but it riveted attention, nor was the tension relaxed until the blinded king had groped his way out through the heavy rear curtains.

Yeats's *Œdipus the King* is not only great, it is magnificent. While preserving the required atmosphere of the classic drama, he has also imparted to the play the qualities which make it appeal to a modern audience. He has, incidentally, presented theatres of the "little" kind with a drama which should retain a permanent place in the repertory of community groups, and he has brought Greek classic drama within the reach and understanding of audiences to whom it has heretofore represented the highest standard of intellectuality. Little and Community theatres all over the English-speaking world have been provided with a vehicle easy to produce, and it will be very surprising if the new Yeats version will not continue to awe audiences all over the world for the next ten years to come.

Ireland is truly a strange country, and the versatility of her people is equally strange. What is said of them to-day in truth ceases to be true to-morrow. But yesterday it was said that the Abbey audiences had degenerated and that they revelled only in the sordid and in the farcical. This week they proved themselves more than appreciative of the sublime in drama. Yesterday it was declared that the Abbey players were so drilled in the gait of the Irish peasant and so steeped in the peasant accent that it was impossible for them to cast either aside and be even ordinary human beings upon the stage.

In *Œdipus the King* they separated themselves completely from their Abbey Theatre selves, and, in gait, gesture, and accent, they became majestic. Disguise themselves as they would in modern plays, the veil was penetrated by the eye, while the ear caught unfailingly the familiar individual characteristics of each speaker. But in this Greek tragedy it was not possible to pick out who was who without referring to the programme.

Was it deliberate or just mere coincidence that Shaw's *The Shewing up of Blanco Posnet* was included in the programme with the Greek tragedy? The scenes of enthusiasm which greeted the Shaw play on its first production many years ago came nearest to those which took place this week. It must be confessed, however, that, after the Sophocles-Yeats work, Shaw fell somewhat flat. Nevertheless, the two plays presented a contrast in that each presented different ideas about the attitude of God toward human beings. It may be treason in the eyes of some to compare Shaw with Sophocles, but the fact remains that these two plays, one by a most ancient author and the other by a modern writer who is still living, are comments on Divine Justice as well as upon human interpretation thereof and submission thereto.

2.—*New Plays and Old.*

The year 1927 is remarkable for the number of new plays, beginning with Lady Gregory's adaptation of Cervantes' " Don Quixote" entitled *Sancho's Master,* on Monday, March 14, 1927. In this play she succeeds to a certain extent in condensing the incidents of this extensive novel into three acts. Many splendid interpretations of the various characters were given, but the one that stood out most prominently was Mr. F. J. McCormick's rendering of Don Quixote, his portrayal of the unhappy Don being truly superb.

A very warm welcome greeted *Parted,* by Mr. M. C. Madden, on April 5, 1927. It is described as a one-act tragedy. The plot is slight in structure, but withal has some very clever dialogue and a sound dramatic climax. Mr. Michael Dolan scored one of the hits of his varied career as Tom Morris, the embittered old farmer. Mr. F. J. McCormick again displayed his talents in a different rôle. Mr. Michael Scott and Miss Shelah Richards gave pleasing performances. Both these young players are at present playing in America and getting some very fine notices. May 9th saw the première of *Dave,* by Lady Gregory whose pen is busy with her prolific works. This little one-act play smacks of Dickens's " Haunted Man." It is a wonderful little piece full of dramatic studies. Mr. J. Stephenson did good work as Dave and gave a convincing study. He has quite a reputation for clear enunciation, a very desirable quality in an actor. Mr. Michael Dolan generally pays much attention to his make-up, and his character studies are very remarkable, his Nicholas O'Cahan in this play being very convincing. Miss Maureen Delany, who reminds me very much of the great Sara Allgood, gave a good account of herself in the part of Mrs. O'Cahan. May 16th was selected for the production of *Black Oliver,* a play in one act by John Guinan. This play deals with ghosts, is cleverly written, and was well received.

On July 28 *Cathleen ni Houlihan* was revived by W. B. Yeats. Later on Eugene O'Neill, the much talked of American author, had the honour of having his play, *Emperor Jones,* produced at the Abbey by the Dublin Drama League, and having it added to the renowned Abbey's already extensive repertoire. Mr. Rutherford Mayne of Belfast made a sensational success as Brutus and was recalled five times before the curtain. Monday, September

12, *Œdipus at Colonus,* W. B. Yeats's version of Sophocles' tragedy, was produced to a capacity house. The entire audience sat enthralled for over two hours listening in awed silence. Mr. F. J. McCormick again played Œdipus the King and carried the honours of the evening. His portrayal of the old blind man was a triumph that any actor might be justly proud of. And Mr. Michael Dolan, the reliable, created quite an impression by his manliness and dignity, as did Mr. Barry Fitzgerald as Creon. Mr. J. Stephenson again charmed by his singing and clear enunciation.

On October 3rd, Mr. Lennox Robinson added another to his long list of successes as a producer, presenting *The Pipe in the Fields,* by Mr. T. C. Murray. Mr. Murray's plays are always regarded as events of importance, and *The Pipe* was no exception. On the rise of the curtain there was no spare standing or sitting-room. A record audience was in attendance to see the new play by this gifted author. No one was disappointed, and *The Pipe in the Fields* set the seal on Mr. Murray's already established reputation. In this play Mr. Michael Dolan left a deep impression by his playing of the part of Father Moore, and no character of his handling has ever been better done.

CHAPTER XVI.

The Year 1928.

1.—*The Silver Tassie.*

MUCH interest was occasioned in the spring of 1928 by the Abbey's rejection of a new play by Seán O'Casey. In London, where he had now made his home, he had been accorded the welcome due to a literary celebrity. He had been fêted and lionized. But not a few of his friends feared that in quitting Dublin he had left his material and his inspiration behind him and might never find them anywhere else.

Confirmation of their fears appeared when a majority of the Abbey directors decided that his *Silver Tassie,* a tragi-comedy in four acts dealing with the Great War, fell definitely below the high level he had attained in *The Plough and the Stars.* O'Casey, said Yeats, was not really interested in the Great War; he had never stood on its battlefields, or walked its hospitals; hence his failure to make a good play about it. This dictum that a dramatist must write wholly out of his personal experience struck O'Casey as a piece of Yeatsian absurdity that must not go unchallenged. In the correspondence that followed, and was subsequently communicated to the Press, the dramatist hit out with a great deal of bitter force in his own defence, while his judges, manifestly ill at ease, sought to disarm his resentment by rather vainly complimenting the author on the excellence of his earlier work.

What particularly irritated O'Casey, however, was the manner in which it was proposed to reject his play. In view of his recognized genius, his strong popular appeal, and the fact—admitted by Yeats— that to him more than to any other dramatist in recent times the Abbey owed its success, it was not without considerable reluctance that the Directors decided on rejection. It was an invidious thing, as it seemed to them, that the Abbey, which had given O'Casey to the world, should now be known to have struck a blow at his prestige. Accordingly, with what proved to be a wholly unwelcome exercise of tact, Yeats got Lady Gregory to write to the author suggesting that he should withdraw his play "for revision," or write to say he had become dissatisfied with it and ask it back.

O'Casey's reply was characteristic: "I am too big for this sort of mean and petty shuffling. There is going to be no damned secrecy with me surrounding the Abbey's rejection of the play. A well-known English manager, who thinks the play a good one, has been considering a London producer."

The author recovered his manuscript, and *The Silver Tassie* was shortly afterwards published in book form. It still awaits its stage production.

2.—*A Remarkable Repertoire.*

Some idea of the variety and extent of the Abbey Company's repertoire may be got from the fact that in the year 1928 no fewer than forty-four plays were presented. Eight of these were new to the Abbey stage, the most important being Brinsley Mac-Namara's *The Master* (March 6), T. C. Murray's *The Blind Wolf* (April 30), and Lennox Robinson's *The Far-off Hills* (October 22). Ibsen's *John Gabriel Borkman* was staged on April 3; while on November 6 the company produced Shakespeare's *Lear*.

Of the plays that were not new the majority were well-established favourites whose names have figured so frequently in the preceding pages that detailed mention of them is not necessary. It would perhaps be not unfair to assume that the Abbey directors, having as good artists trained their audiences to enjoy only excellent work, now as good business men believe in giving them the excellent work that they enjoy most. If one may judge from the number of performances allotted to the several plays in the year under review, the dramatists that are most popular with the Abbey's patrons are: T. C. Murray, Seán O'Casey, Bernard Shaw, and Brinsley MacNamara.

To glance down the official list of the year's productions—old and new—is to form some slight conception of the strenuous life of the repertory actor. For each actor to be word-perfect in so many rôles; to portray, with no obvious diminution of freshness and enthusiasm, so many and so diverse characters; to lose, as it were, his own

identity and yet retain firm hold on all his accumu-
lated skill, this week in a drama of the Connacht
peasantry, next week in one of ancient Thebes, and
the week after that, perhaps, in an uproarious
comedy of suburban Dublin: all this demands an
efficiency and a versatile scope not always realized
by even the most appreciative audience.

CHAPTER XVII.

KEEPING IN TOUCH WITH THE ORIGINAL IRISH PLAYERS.

MENTION has been made in an earlier chapter of Mr. Sinclair's severance of his connexion with the National Theatre Society, and of his formation of an independent company, the Irish Players. That breach was, unfortunately, complete, and the work of the Irish Players falls definitely outside the Abbey's story. Yet to that story in its earlier stages Sinclair and Maire O'Neill contributed so much that a brief account of their subsequent activities may be forgiven and even welcomed.

In October 1916 the Sinclair Irish Players returned to their native Dublin, not to the Abbey but to the Gaiety Theatre, and played there with great success. An engagement from the management of the Empire Theatre, Dublin, was offered them to appear in *Duty*, by Seamus O'Brien. The Abbey Theatre directors immediately got busy and started an injunction to restrain Mr. Sinclair from playing *Duty*, to protect the rights which they held to the piece. Mr. Sinclair was summoned to appear before the Master of the Rolls, who, on hearing the facts set forth by Mr. Sinclair, refused to grant the injunction sought for, but asked Mr. Sinclair to agree not to play

Duty beyond that present week, to which Mr. Sinclair readily agreed. The Abbey directors dropped the case, and *Duty* was again played the following year in Dublin by the Sinclair Company. About this time or a little later Mr. Sinclair met Mr. James Fagan who had written a one-act play *Doctor O'Toole* to fit the entire company of Irish players, and it was booked by the former Abbey Theatre agents for a tour of the English Music Halls or Vaudeville Houses. *Doctor O'Toole* was produced in Cork, January 1917, and was an instantaneous success. From Cork they took *O'Toole* to the Empire Theatre, Liverpool, and from there to the Coliseum, London, where it became such a favourite that it was played over two thousand times.

Their next venture was a rather hazardous and daring one, but it proved to be both an artistic and financial success. Mr. Sinclair took over the entire management of the Court Theatre, London, and played a whole season. *The Playboy of the Western World* was revived, and Miss Maire O'Neill was secured to play her original rôle of Pegeen. At the conclusion of the Court season the company crossed to Ireland, playing two weeks at Belfast and two at Cork. Mr. Sinclair now entered into partnership with Walter McNally, the famous Irish singer, and formed a company of Irish artists to play the Music Halls in Scotland, playing Aberdeen, Glasgow, and Edinburgh, which took them into the month of July. In August they started a real Irish tour of small and large towns, finishing in Dublin just before Christmas. The end of this year,

1918, found them back again in England in the Music Halls, alternating with *O'Toole* and *Duty* with continued success and growing popularity.

On St. Patrick's Day, 1919, they appeared at the Gaiety Theatre, Dublin, whence they returned immediately to England and ran there up to the end of Holy Week, finishing at Southampton. They crossed to Dublin on Sunday, and opened a tour at New Ross, County Wexford, on Easter Monday, 1919. On May 22, Mr. Sinclair received a wire telling him of his mother's death. He hastened to Dublin, spending three days there, and returning to Ballinasloe to resume work up to the middle of July, when they took a well-earned rest for a few weeks. It was during this tour that the following incident took place:—

In 1919 when the Players were on tour in Ireland their best support came from the English military. In Claremorris the only person who could be found to play the piano for the rebel song called for by *The Eloquent Dempsey* was an English officer. He asked only that a screen be placed so that he could not be seen by the audience. When the Irish Players started the song the Irish in the gallery joined in most heartily because of the English officers and their wives in the stalls:

Soldiers are we,
Whose lives are pledged to Ireland;
Some have come from a land beyond the wave,
Sworn to be free,
No more our ancient sireland
Shall shelter the despot or the slave...

And then a fellow-officer kicked over the screen. The Irish cheered, the English laughed, and the pianist fled, fearful of what his commanding officer would say. But the Colonel went behind the stage to say: "Remember, Mr. Sinclair, I wasn't here to-night!"

They opened again in Galway during August race week and continued up to January 1920, without leaving Ireland. At this time they crossed to London to appear at the Victoria Palace Theatre, then made a tour through the English provinces playing the Music Halls into April of this year.

Returning to Dublin they played at the Empire and also made a picture for the Film Company of Ireland, entitled *Paying the Rent,* in which Arthur Sinclair starred. It was a tremendous success and was exhibited all over Ireland. Towards the middle of August the company went to London to rehearse *The Whiteheaded Boy,* by Lennox Robinson. Mr. James B. Fagan had secured the rights of production with the idea of having Miss Sara Allgood in the cast and of securing the entire company of original Irish Players.

Miss Allgood was in Australia at this time; Mr. Fagan cabled her offering the engagement, and Miss Allgood replied accepting the offer, and saying that she would start for London immediately. On September 13, 1920, the old original Irish Players reassembled and opened in Manchester with *The Whiteheaded Boy,* playing a two-weeks' engagement there. Then journeying to London they opened at the Ambassador's Theatre on September 27. *The Whiteheaded Boy* became an instantaneous success and ran there for a complete year, playing extra matinées, and giving nine performances weekly. About this time the Stage Society of London put on *O'Flaherty, V.C.,* by George Bernard Shaw at the Lyric Theatre, Hammersmith, for special performances. At the request of Mr. Shaw, Arthur Sinclair played O'Flaherty; Sara Allgood, Mrs. O'Flaherty; Miss Nan Fitzgerald, O'Flaherty's sweetheart; and Mr. Roy Byford, the General. The production was received with popular acclaim.

In September 1922, the Irish Players, with the exception of Sara Allgood, who remained in London, left for a tour of the principal cities of America under the management of Charles Dillingham, making their fourth visit to the States. They then sailed for Australia, remaining there seven months playing the various cities with indifferent success. They were back again in London in 1923, crossed over to Ireland, and played for a few months.

Sara Allgood was touring the English provinces in *The Whiteheaded Boy,* and Arthur Sinclair joined the company to play his old part. About this time Mr. Sinclair received an offer by wire from Mr. L. C. Dagnall to play with the famous Sir Charles Hawtrey in *Send for Doctor O'Grady,* by George Birmingham, the author of *General John Regan.* Mr. Sinclair accepted the engagement and went up to London for rehearsals. *Send for Dr. O'Grady* was produced in July and was an outstanding success.

On Monday night while Sir Charles was waiting in the wings for his entrance he said to Mr. Sin-

clair: "Barring a vistation from Providence, this
play will run a year." The words were prophetic.
That night a friend came to the theatre to see
Mr. Sinclair, and, while they were speaking, Sir
Charles went by and patting Sinclair on the back
as he passed him, said, "Goodbye." The following
day, Tuesday, at the matinée, Sir Charles was ill,
and on the following Monday he was dead. Mr.
Sinclair and Miss Maire O'Neill, who was also in
the cast, bought the rights of the play, and while
waiting to assemble a suitable cast they took a
turn through the Music Halls with a playlet entitled
Special Pleading by Bernard Duffy. Having engaged
a suitable cast for *Send for Dr. O'Grady,* they
started out on a tour of the English provinces, and
while playing Southampton Mr. Sinclair received a
cable from Mr. Henry Miller of New York offering
him a part in a play which was ready for production.
Mr. Sinclair immediately accepted Mr. Miller's offer,
and cancelling his English engagements sailed for
America in January 1924, where he created the part
of Seamus O'Tandy in *The Merry Wives of Gotham*
at the Henry Miller Theatre in New York. When
Mr. Sinclair arrived for rehearsals in this play, he
discovered that the character he was to portray
bore the rather doubtful name of O'Briskey, which
amused him very much. He told the author that
there was never such a name in Ireland. The
author explained that it was a name coined to rhyme
with "whiskey." Here Mr. Sinclair broke into a
loud laugh and asked if any other spirit would do;
the author said that it would, so Mr. Sinclair

L

changed the "whiskey" to "brandy" and gave the character the name of Seamus O'Tandy.

At the end of the New York run Mr. Sinclair returned to London and went into a short play or sketch playing an Irish part with an English company. Finishing this engagement in Preston, England, January 1925, he returned to London where he produced *Persevering Pat* under Archibald de Bear's management with the original company. The play was not a great success, but it managed to run for a time. He next played at the Olympia Theatre, Dublin, then returned with the whole company to London, and made an eight weeks' tour of the provinces. After this he returned to London again to the Brough Stratford, September 1925. Two weeks later they appeared under the management of Mr. James B. Fagan and Mr. Denis Eadie at the Royalty Theatre in a revival of *The Playboy of the Western World,* which played for five weeks. In November they produced Seán O'Casey's *Juno and the Paycock,* with Sara Allgood in her original part of Juno and followed this in 1926 with O'Casey's *Plough and the Stars.*

Between the Royalty, the New, and the Fortune Theatres they played practically a year; six months of *Juno,* five of *The Plough,* and one of *The Playboy.* On June 26 Miss Maire O'Neill and Mr. Arthur Sinclair were married in Corpus Christi Chapel, Maiden Lane, London, by the Rev. Father James Kearney. The witnesses were Miss Cynthia Stockley and Miss Sara Allgood.

In September of 1926 they went on tour with *Juno* until December, finishing in Birmingham, and the following Monday opened at the Criterion Theatre, London, with *The Whiteheaded Boy,* which they played for six weeks. *Juno* was revived, and the company transferred from the Criterion Theatre to the Vaudeville, where they put on *Professor Tim,* by George Shiels. Then they moved over to the Court Theatre and produced *The Shadow of a Gunman,* by Seán O'Casey, with *Riders to the Sea,* by J. M. Synge, as another attraction. At the conclusion of the Court season *Juno* was again put on tour. It was on this occasion that Miss Maire O'Neill played the part of Juno for the first time and made one of the outstanding successes of her career, her sister, Sara Allgood, having gone to the Palace Theatre to play in *The Girl Friend.*

The *Juno* tour finished in November at the Hippodrome, Lewisham. This was their final engagement this year in England. Mr. George C. Tyler had booked them for an engagement in America, and they sailed on the "Laurentic" to open at the Hudson Theatre, New York, November 28, 1927, in *The Plough and the Stars,* which was played to a little hissing, but on the whole to an enthusiastic audience who applauded them so insistently at the end that the entire company took ten curtain calls. They played four weeks at this theatre with marked success to an evening-dress audience. The popular parts of the house were beginning to fill up just as they were compelled to move up town to the new Gallo Theatre. Here they produced *Juno* to a packed house and large audiences prevailed here for the three weeks' stay.

Moving over to the Knickerbocker, they continued
to do good business with *The Plough* and *Juno*
alternately. The following criticism by Miss Elizabeth Jordan sums up the situation graphically: —

The Irish Players are here, bless them—here with
their rich Irish brogue and their keen Irish wit and
their sharp Irish tongues and their quick Irish fists
and their brilliant Irish gifts of mimicry. Here,
too, are the Irish audiences that gather to see them
in the plays they have brought over, and here are
the non-Irish spectators (poor things) who have
gathered to see audiences and players lose their
tempers and make an Irish holiday.

Thus far no blood has been shed—perhaps to the
artless disappointment of all—but there is some
hissing where too much stress is laid on unamiable
Irish characteristics. When the noble traits of the
Irish are shown, everybody takes them calmly and
acquiescently, as well they may. We all know the
Irish are full of noble traits. Why certain members
of the audience are displeased when it is hinted that
a few of them also have faults is hard to understand.
We do not get excited when we are shown American
plays with American men and women revealing
their imperfections. As for English plays revealing
the faults of certain English types, we simply love
them! So why—but enough of this. By the time
these thoughtful words are in type the policemen
who have been guarding the Hudson Theater and
the Gallo Theater to prevent outbreaks in the
audiences will be back on their beats with reminis-
cent grins on their lips and the memory of some
fine acting in their hearts—and that is all there is
to that.

This being so, it may be admitted that the Irish
Players were rather unfortunate in the choice of
their first play for the New York season. Seán
O'Casey's *The Plough and the Stars* is a powerful
but depressing piece of work, and even the vigorous

and humorous tongue-lashing that goes on between the two leading women characters, Bessie Burgess and Mrs. Gogan (superbly played by Sara Allgood and Maire O'Neill) is not enough to raise the spirits of the audience. But that audience sees a magnificent bit of acting in the death of Bessie Burgess; and the scene in which she folds an old shawl across her breast and goes forth to face British artillery in behalf of a suffering woman who needs a doctor is "one of those moments" on the stage. However, a play that offers us two violent deaths, one case of galloping consumption, and one case of insanity, does not quite fit into the gaiety of the Yuletide season. Neither does the Irish Players' next attraction *Juno and the Paycock,* which is equally powerful and equally depressing. What American audiences want from these brilliant artists —by way of variety at least—is some Celtic playwriting as sincere as O'Casey's, but with hope and beauty in it in addition to his strength and sincerity. Here is looking forward to the day we get it.[1]

On February 6 they opened at the Broad Street Theatre and were enthusiastically received. If Philadelphians were trying to redeem their past reception of the then Abbey Players in 1911, when they had them arrested for playing *The Playboy,* they succeeded, for not in the history of the Irish Players' visits to America have they had such a magnificent reception. They had come to America expecting much opposition with the O'Casey plays, but with the exception of one or two slight protests in the theatre the tour turned out to be a triumphal march from New York to Philadelphia and Chicago. Enthusiastic audiences hailed plays and players everywhere. Many receptions, dances, and ban-

[1] Elizabeth Jordan in *America,* Jan. 7, 1928.

quets were given in their honour, and in each city
they were fêted and dined.

Some one suggested that the Irish Players should
give an " Actors' Benefit," not to help indigent
players but to give the profession a few tips on the
art of acting. Mr. Arthur B. Waters, writing in the
Philadelphia Public Ledger of the actors in *The
Plough and the Stars,* says: —

Last night's performance glowed and burned with
a steady flame; such old favourites as Arthur
Sinclair, Sara Allgood, and Maire O'Neill, reinforced
by a number of new faces, breathed the breath of
ruddy life into their characters, and gave the
dialogue, much of it brilliant and imaginative as
Irish dramatists invariably know how to make their
dialogue, every inflection and shading and degree
of richness that it deserved.[2]

The reception accorded to the Irish Players at the
Blackstone Theatre, Chicago, was marvellous. I
give two criticisms which speak volumes:

The Plough and the Stars itself is a treasure from
the most flaming pen that Ireland has produced
since John Millington Synge lighted the stage like a
flambeau. The words of O'Casey's characters are
like strings of crystal, he limns a figure with an
etcher's fineness, economy, and exactitude of line,
and his feeling for and management of the
dramatic incident and scene are splendid and true.
The leading figures of his play hang upon the rim
of the violent short-lived rebellion and are sucked
into it now and again, some to suffer its tragic
consequences, others to serve as mere observers
and reporters of its sanguinary scenes. But through-

[2] Arthur B. Waters, in *The Phila. Public Ledger,* Feb. 7,
1928.

out the turmoil and the peril this paradoxical thing known as human nature is revealed in its weakness as well as in its strength, in its folly and sordidness as well as in its depth and its divine capacity for sacrifice.

In this rare play the priceless Arthur Sinclair has come back to act as a Dublin loafer, straddler of issues, and vocally combative ne'er-do-well; the great Sara Allgood has returned to personate a rum-swigging fruit-vendor with a son in the world-war and with leaning toward the rule of the British throne; Maire O'Neill to represent with extraordinary clarity and interest the complex nature of a loquacious charwoman; Sydney Morgan to play a shallowly keen socialist and laborite; J. A. O'Rourke to act a vacillating and quarrelsome old patriot; Cathleen Drago to picture a woman of the streets with as much truth as if she had just stepped in from the pavement, and Harry Hutchinson to act a chicken-butcher turned captain of the Citizen Army.[3]

The following appeared in the " Chicago Daily Journal," on February 23, 1928: —

The most notable enterprise of its kind in the world in this century has been the Abbey Theater of Dublin. From the stage of that playhouse sprang the Irish renaissance, and its support of a characteristic Milesian drama has called forth a great number of plays of the highest merit—some of them, indeed, works of positive genius. And on that stage grew up, from an amateur beginning, a company which for truth in the representation of character and for excellence of ensemble is not excelled, if it is matched, anywhere in the world. These Irish Players, who were first assembled twenty-two years ago, have ardently pursued their purpose all this long time and, while making no pretence to

[3] Virginia Dale, in the *Chicago Daily Journal,* Feb. 21, 1928.

superiority, they stand to-day supreme. In revisiting Chicago and staging the plays of Seán O'Casey they offer proof that they have steadily gone ahead since last they were here. They are among the glories of the theater, and they increase the glory of their race.[4]

Returning to Ireland from their American triumphs, Arthur Sinclair and Maire O'Neill (Mrs. Sinclair), went to Dublin and immediately began rehearsals of *The Real McCoy,* a comedy in three acts by M. J. J. MacKeown, which was produced at the Olympia Theatre, Dublin, on June 25th, 1928, and played to packed houses for two weeks. The play met with a great reception; so also did Sinclair and Miss O'Neill, who were welcomed home to the city of their birth where they have endeared themselves to the hearts of Dublin's playgoers. On July 9th they started a tour of the English provinces with the same play, opening at the Grand Theatre, Blackpool, and have been playing since that time, with the exception of a flying trip through vaudeville for a period of five weeks—four weeks at the London Coliseum, and one week at the Manchester Hippodrome. In the beginning of 1929 they began a tour of the principal Irish towns which finished on March 9th, then over to London where they began rehearsals of Seán O'Casey's plays *Juno and the Paycock, The Plough and the Stars,* and *The Shadow of a Gunman.* Arthur Sinclair now holds the exclusive rights of these three plays from the author, Seán O'Casey.

On March 18th Sinclair and his Irish Players started out on a tour of the principal cities of Eng-

---

[4] Editorial in the *Chicago Daily Journal* Feb 23, 1928.

land, Scotland, and Wales, playing _The Real McCoy,_ March 18, at the Lyceum Theatre, Newport; March 25, Grand Theatre, Swansea; April 1, Pavilion Theatre, Penzance; April 8, Embassy Theatre, London; April 15, Empire Theatre, Manchester; April 22, Empire Theatre, Wood Green, London. At the termination of this engagement they took up the O'Casey plays, opening on April 29 at the Winter Gardens, Blackpool; May 6, Prince of Wales Theatre, Birmingham; May 13, King's Theatre, Glasgow; May 20, King's Theatre, Edinburgh; May 27, Royal Court Theatre, Liverpool.

At this point I must leave the Irish Players to continue their journey. The printer is calling for copy so that this humble story of mine may be out in time for the twenty-fifth birthday of the Abbey.

I realize that I have fallen short in my attempt to give an accurate account of the Abbey Theatre, its Plays and Players. But I can say that I have done my best to get all the details concerning the foundation and growth of this great literary and dramatic movement, and no man can do more. It was at times a very difficult matter to secure the necessary data, being so far away from Ireland, and from those who have any connexion with the theatre in its twenty-five years of existence.

I wish to thank sincerely all those who have helped me in the making of the book, and if it serves any purpose towards enlightening the minds of those interested in the Irish people and their drama, it will not have been written in vain.

" The last thing in making a book is to know what to put first." I hope that I have started at the right place—I know that I have ended there.

—REV. DAWSON BYRNE, M.A.

U.S.A.

APPENDIX A

A List of Plays produced by the National Theatre Society, Limited, in the Abbey Theatre, with the dates of their first productions there:—

ANON.

The Interlude of Youth	1911
The Second Shepherd's Play	1911
The Annunciation ...	1912
The Flight into Egypt	1912
The Worlde and the Chylde	1912

A. AND O.

Blight	1917

JOHN BARNEWALL.

The Bacac	1917

E. F. BARRETT.

The Grabber	1918

F. BARRINGTON.

The Daeman in the House	1920

W. SCAWEN BLUNT.

Fand	1907

WILLIAM BOYLE.

The Building Fund ...	1905
The Eloquent Dempsey	1906
The Mineral Workers...	1906
Family Failing	1912
Nic	1916

M. M. BRENNAN.

The Young Man from Rathmines	1922
A Lepraucaun in the Tenement	1922

G. BROSNAN.

Before Midnight ...	1928

C. CALLISTER.

A Little Bit of Youth ...	1918

JOSEPH CAMPBELL.

Judgment	1912

W. F. CASEY.

The Man who Missed the Tide	1908
The Suburban Groove...	1908

SADIE CASEY.

Brady	1919

R. A. CHRISTIE.

The Dark Hour ...	1914

PADRAIC COLUM.

The Land	1905
The Fiddler's House ...	1907
Thomas Muskerry ...	1910
Grasshopper	1922

JOSEPH CONNOLLY.

The Mine Land	1913

DANIEL CORKERY.

The Labour Leader ...	1919
The Yellow Bittern ...	1920

WILLIAM CRONE.

The Bargain	1915

MAURICE DALTON.

Sable and Gold ...	1918

S. R. DAY AND G. D. CUMMINS.

Broken Faith	1913
Fox and Geese	1917

BERNARD DUFFY.

Fraternity	1916
The Coiner	1916
The Counter Charm ...	1916
The Piper of Tavran...	1921

LORD DUNSANY.

The Glittering Gate ...	1909
King Argimenes and The	
Unknown Warrior ...	1911
A Night at an Inn ...	1919
The Tents of the Arabs	1920

ST. JOHN G. ERVINE.

Mixed Marriage ...	1911
The Magnanimous Lover	1912
The Critics	1913
The Orangeman ...	1914
John Ferguson ...	1915
The Island of Saints ...	1920

H. FARJEON.

Friends	1917

W. R. FEARON AND ROY NESBITT.

When Love Came Over	
the Hills	1918

DESMOND FITZGERALD.

The Saint	1919

GEORGE FITZMAURICE.

The Country Dress-	
maker	1907
The Piedish ...	1908
The Magic Glasses ...	1913
'Twixt the Giltinans	
and the Carmodys ...	1923

OLIVER GOLDSMITH.

The Goodnatured Man...	1920
She Stoops to Conquer	1923

LADY GREGORY.

Spreading the News ...	1904
Kincora	1905
The White Cockade ...	1905
Hyacinth Halvey ...	1906
The Gaol Gate	1906
The Canavans	1906
The Rising of the Moon	1907
The Jackdaw	1907
Dervorgilla	1907
The Workhouse Ward	1908
The Image	1909
The Travelling Man ...	1910
The Full Moon	1910
Coats	1910
The Deliverer	1911
McDonough's Wife ...	1912
Damer's Gold	1912
Shanwalla	1915
Hanrahan's Oath ...	1918
The Dragon	1919
The Bogie Men ...	1920
The Golden Apple ...	1921
Aristotle's Bellows ...	1921
The Story Brought by	
Brigit	1924
Sancho's Master ...	1927
Dave	1927

LADY GREGORY AND DR. DOUGLAS HYDE.

The Poorhouse	1907

J. GUINAN.

The Cuckoo's Nest ...	1913
The Plough-lifters ...	1916
Black Oliver	1927

ELIZABETH HARTE.

Mr. Murphy's Island ... 1926

F. JAY.

The Cobweb 1914

D. L. KELLEHER.

Stephen Grey 1909

MRS. BART KENNEDY.

My Lord 1913

W. M. LETTS.

The Eyes of the Blind	1907
The Challenge	1909

M. C. MADDEN.

Parted 1927

DOROTHY MACARDLE.

Atonement	1918
Ann Kavanagh ...	1922
The Old Man	1925

THOMAS MACDONAGH.

When the Dawn is Come 1908

BRINSLEY MACNAMARA.

The Rebellion in Bally-cullen	1919
The Land for the People	1920
The Glorious Uncertainty	1923
The Master	1928

TERENCE MACSWINEY.

The Revolutionist ... 1921

J. BERNARD MACCARTHY.

Kinship	1914
The Supplanter ...	1914
The Crusaders	1917
The Long Road to Garranbraher ...	1923

M. J. MCHUGH.

A Minute's Wait ...	1914
The Philosopher ...	1915
Tommy Tom-Tom ...	1917

ROSE MCKENNA.

Aliens 1918

EDWARD MCNULTY.

The Lord Mayor ...	1914
The Courting of Mary Doyle	1921

D. C. MAHER.

Partition 1916

RUTHERFORD MAYNE.

Red Turf 1911

F. C. MOORE AND W. P. FLANAGAN.

By Word of Mouth ... 1915

STEPHEN MORGAN.

The Serf 1920

T. C. MURRAY.

Birthright	1910
Maurice Harte	1912
Sovereign Love ...	1913
Spring	1918
Aftermath	1922
Autumn Fire	1924
The Piper in the Fields	1927
The Blind Wolf ...	1928

K. O'BRENNAN.

Full Measure 1928

SEUMAS O'BRIEN.

Duty	1913

SEAN O'CASEY.

The Shadow of a Gun-man	1923
Cathleen Listens In ...	1923
Juno and the Paycock	1924
Nannie's Night Out ...	1924
The Plough and the Stars	1926

F. J. H. O'DONNELL.

The Drifters	1920
Anti-Christ	1925

FAND O'GRADY.

Apartments	1923

SEUMAS O'KELLY.

The Shuiler's Child ...	1910
The Bribe	1913
The Parnellite	1917
Meadowsweet	1919

CON O'LEARY.

The Crossing	1914
Queer Ones	1919

EUGENE O'NEILL.

Emperor Jones ...	1927

FERGUS O'NOLAN.

A Royal Alliance ...	1920

CONAL O'RIORDAN (NORREYS CONNELL).

The Piper	1908
Time	1909
An Imaginary Conver-sation	1909

GIDEON OUSELY.

A Serious Thing ...	1919
The Enchanted Trousers	1919

G. SIDNEY PATERNOSTER.

The Dean of St. Pat-rick's	1913

VICTOR O'D. POWER.

David Mahony	1913

R. J. PURCELL.

The Spoiling of Wilson	1917

K. F. PURDON.

Candle and Crib ...	1920

R. J. RAY.

The White Feather ...	1909
The Casting out of Martin Whelan ...	1910
The Gombeen Man ...	1913
The Strong Hand ...	1917
The Moral Law ...	1922

WALTER RIDDELL.

The Prodigal	1914

GERTRUDE ROBINS.

The Home Coming ...	1913

LENNOX ROBINSON.

The Clancy Name ...	1908
The Cross Roads ...	1909
Harvest	1910
Patriots	1912
The Dreamers	1915
The Whiteheaded Boy	1916
The Lost Leader ...	1918
The Round Table ...	1922
Crabbed Youth and Age	1922
Never the Time and the Place	1924
Portrait	1925
The White Blackbird	1925
The Far-off Hills ...	1928

W. P. RYAN.

The Jug of Sorrow ...	1914

KENNETH SARR.

| The Passing | ... | ... | 1924 |
| Old Mag | ... | ... | 1924 |

SHAKESPEARE.

| King Lear | ... | ... | 1928 |

G. B. SHAW.

The Shewing Up of Blanco Posnet	...	1909
John Bull's Other Island	... ...	1916
Widowers' Houses	...	1916
Arms and the Man	...	1916
Man and Superman	...	1917
The Doctor's Dilemma		1917
The Inca of Perusalem		1917
The Devil's Disciple	...	1920
The Man of Destiny	...	1922
Fanny's First Play	...	1925

RICHARD BRINSLEY SHERIDAN.

| The Scheming Lieutenant | ... ... | 1908 |
| The Critic | ... ... | 1914 |

GEORGE SHIELS.

Bedmates	...	...	1921
Insurance Money	...	1921
Paul Twyning	...	...	1922
First Aid	...	1923
The Retrievers	...	...	1924
Professor Tim	...	1925

JAMES STEPHENS.

| The Wooing of Julia Elizabeth | ... | 1920 |

J. M. SYNGE.

The Well of the Saints	1905
The Playboy of the Western World	...	1907
Deirdre of the Sorrows	1910

RABINDRANATH TAGORE.

| The Post Office | ... | 1913 |

A. PATRICK WILSON.

| The Cobbler | ... | ... | 1914 |
| The Slough | ... | ... | 1914 |

W. B. YEATS.

On Baile's Strand	...	1904
Deirdre	...	...	1906
The Shadowy Waters (Rev. version)	...	1906
The Golden Helmet	...	1908
The Green Helmet	...	1910
The Land of Heart's Desire	... ...	1911
The Countess Cathleen (Rev. version)	...	1912
The King's Threshold (Rev. version)	...	1913
The Player Queen	...	1919
Œdipus the King	...	1926
Œdipus at Colonus	...	1927

W. B. YEATS AND LADY GREGORY.

| The Unicorn from the Stars | ... ... | 1907 |

TRANSLATIONS.

The Doctor in Spite of Himself (Molière)	...	1906
Interior (Maeterlinck)	...	1907
Teja (Sudermann)	...	1908
The Rogueries of Scapin (Molière)	... ...	1908
The Miser (Molière)	...	1909
Mirandolina (Goldoni)	...	1910
Nativity Play (Hyde)	...	1911
Marriage, The (Hyde)		1911
Hannele (Hauptmann)		1913
There are Crimes and Crimes (Strindberg)	...	1913
The Stronger (Strindberg)	... ...	1913
A Perfect Day (Mazaud)	1921
A Merry Death (Evreinov)	... ...	1921
A Doll's House (Ibsen)	1923
The Two Shepherds (Sierra)	... ...	1924

TRANSLATIONS.—continued.

The Kingdom of God
(Sierra)   1924
The Proposal (Tche-
chov)   1925
Œdipus (Sophocles)   ...   1926

TRANSLATIONS.—continued.

John Gabriel Borkman
(Ibsen)   1928
*The Women Have Their
Way* (Quintero)   ...   1928

*The following Plays had been produced by the
National Theatre Society and its predecessors before
the opening of the Abbey Theatre:—*

" A. E."
Deirdre   1902

PADRAIC COLUM.
Broken Soil   1903

LADY GREGORY.
Twenty-five   1903

DOUGLAS HYDE.
Casadh an t-Sugáin   ...   1901

EDWARD MARTYN.
The Heather Field   ...   1899
Maeve   1900

SEUMAS MACMANUS.
*The Townland of Tam-
ney*   1904

ALICE MILLIGAN.
*The Last Feast of the
Fianna*   1900

GEORGE MOORE.
*The Bending of the
Bough*   1900

SEUMAS O'CUISIN.
The Sleep of the King 1902
The Racing Lug   ...   1902

FRED RYAN.
*The Laying of the Foun-
dations*   1902

J. M. SYNGE.
*In the Shadow of the
Glen*   1903
Riders to the Sea   ...   1904

W. B. YEATS.
The Countess Cathleen   1899
Cathleen ni Houlihan...   1902
A Pot of Broth   1902
The Hour Glass   ...   1903
The King's Threshold   1903
The Shadowy Waters...   1904

W. B. YEATS AND GEORGE
MOORE.
Diarmuid and Grania ...   1901

APPENDIX B

The Little Theatre Movement in England.

THE year 1903 was scarcely a few days old when there began to appear in the daily papers letters of criticism and protest against the then prevailing conditions of the stage. Authors, actors, and others concerned with the art of the theatre, were clamouring for a National or Subsidised Theatre. A. Wing Pinero, now Sir Arthur Wing Pinero, decried England's lamentable state. Regarding the fate of good plays he said: " In other countries, when a fine play is produced, they do something for it. They preserve it; they take a reasonable amount of pride in it; they do not allow it to lie neglected, forgotten; they take good care that from time to time it shall be displayed as evidence of what they can do in that particular department of art and literature. And there you have, in a nutshell, one of the great uses—I do not, by any means, say the only use—of a theatre, whether established by the State, or by a municipal corporation, or by private munificence, independent of the purely commercial conditions which too frequently govern the Drama in Great Britain."

According to other critics the art of the actor was at a very low ebb, in fact in a deplorable condition, with the few exceptions of the great men of that day.

The cry then arose, "What can be done to help the British stage?"

Lord Lansdowne, the Secretary of State for Foreign Affairs, was asked to furnish some information as to the amount of support given in foreign capitals to the opera and the theatre.

A number of reports were supplied as to the conditions existing in Paris, Berlin, Brussels, Lisbon, St. Petersburg (as it then was), and elsewhere, the general outcome being the discovery that in most of the important centres of national life on the Continent a large amount of assistance, either from the reigning sovereign or from the funds of the municipality, was given to dramatic or musical art. England proved to be an exception to this state of affairs.

Mr. John Hare, the celebrated actor, thought that the time had arrived when those interested in the higher drama took drastic measures to arrest its decay. Managers, he thought, of London's theatres were stuffing the public with a surfeit of musical comedy and sacred temples of the drama were being turned into music halls, to be submerged in the toils of frivolity. The only remedy he could advocate was the endowment of a National Theatre and Conservatoire to rescue the art of the stage from the abyss into which it was falling.

The Conservatoire, he saw, was a crying need in order to teach the very amateurish actors the art of correct speech. It was at times impossible to understand one word they were saying. He deplored the passing of the old stock companies, the only possible training-ground for the young actor, where he learned how to become fully equipped in his art. There should be established a school of acting and an Endowed Theatre in London and in every important city, which should be immune from commercial considerations, and where it would be compulsory to produce from time to time the masterpieces of English authors be they dead or living.

Sir Herbert Beerbohm Tree was at that very time contemplating opening a school of dramatic art in the face of much severe criticism. Some said such a school was absurd because acting could not be taught. Tree believed this himself, but he maintained that something could and should be done to train men how to walk the stage and speak correctly. A man might not be taught how to act, but one could prepare the groundwork, bring order out of chaos, and regulate the conditions out of which an actor might emerge, and remove some of the stumbling-blocks which encumber the would-be actor's path. If there were talent it could be developed; elocution, voice production, gesture, deportment, fencing, dancing, and the principles of oratory could be taught, while the noble heritage of the English language could at least be preserved.

It must be observed that the action of Theatrical Syndicates emphasised the purely commercial aspects of the theatre art, and the only remedy was a school of acting in which pupils could be taught or a Subsidized Theatre or a National Repertory Theatre.

The enquiry, "What can be done to save the British Drama?" did not fall on deaf ears.

Sir Herbert Tree started his school of acting, in which much good work was accomplished, but, to become a pupil of such a school, one should have no small amount of means, especially if one happened to reside outside the City of London. Tree's school did not satisfy the cravings of thousands in London, nor did it set to rest the longings of thousands who lived far away in other English cities and towns. It remained for the Irish Abbey Players of Dublin to set the example and to arouse the enthusiasm of England's young men and women to solve the problem for themselves.

The Abbey Players visited London each year and played the principal provincial cities, and thus paved the way for the beginning of the Little Theatre Movement all over the British Empire—a movement which in recent years has spread rapidly.

There is the Repertory movement, consisting for the most part of professional organizations, whose principal aim is artistic merit and not long runs or tours. Among these are the Leeds Repertory Theatre, J. B. Fagan's Playhouse at Oxford, The Festival Theatre at Cambridge, The Maddernmarket Theatre at Norwich, and the Birmingham Repertory Theatre, of which W. G. Fay is producer. And then there are the amateur Little Theatres, all of which are independent organizations, free from the conservative and hampering conditions of the professional theatre.

There is a freedom for the actor in these Little Theatre groups to develop his talents by playing a variety of parts, that cannot be found in a professional company.

As soon as an actor shows any cleverness in playing a certain style of part in the professional theatre
he is doomed to that style for the rest of his life.
After a time he becomes a one-part actor, and settles
in this groove to his own undoing. The Repertory
Theatre and the purely amateur Little Theatre have
done away with this; they give every man and
woman a chance to play a number of varied parts
and to become, in a word, real actors. That is one
of the principal reasons for the success of the Little
Theatres.

The Little Theatre Movement in America.

SHORTLY after the Dublin Abbey Players' visit to
America in 1914, Little Theatres began to spring up
throughout the country, and at the present time
there are thousands.

Some flourish for a time and then die out, while
others continue successfully. The successful ones
are run by idealists who are full of enthusiasm and
are fired with the ambition that their art succeeds
alone for Art's sake. The unsuccessful ones fail
because their founders and directors cannot resist
the lure of publicity, self-aggrandizement, and gold.
The Little Theatre has proved itself to be essentially
a playhouse of ideals and art, and on these lines
alone can it hope to thrive or succeed. The movement arose in America as did the Abbey Theatre in
Ireland—in artistic revolt against the commercialism
of the professional theatre—and the Little Theatre
has taught a severe lesson to its professional brother.

The Little Theatres of the world owe an incalculable debt to the Abbey. It taught the lesson of united effort, it was essentially a theatre of co-operation where the humblest person in the company was of as much importance as the greatest. In this organization the " star " system did not exist; one was as good as another. The actor, playwright, and director held a place that tended only to the success of the venture, and one was helpless without the other.

The first Little Theatre in America to attract attention and gain recognition was " The Washington Square Players."

This group began their career with a production of *The Glittering Gate,* by Lord Dunsany, which took place in the back room of a little book-store in Greenwich Village, New York.

After this venture they moved into the theatrical district of New York City under the name of " The Washington Square Players. They rented a small theatre with a seating capacity of one hundred, and for a period of two or three years the sophisticated playgoers of the city flocked to this miniature theatre to enjoy and applaud their artistic efforts.

This enterprise outgrowing the place, they made a tremendously successful tour of the country, and on their return to New York they founded their own school of the theatre under the title of " The New York Theatre Guild," and erected a splendid theatre which cost over one million dollars.

The Theatre Guild has succeeded beyond the most sanguine expectations, its actors and authors have become world-famous, and it may be said truly that to-day The Theatre Guild is the most powerful organization of its kind in the world.

A second group was organized in Cape Cod, Massachusetts, as "The Provincetown Players," under the direction of George Cam Cook, who held hard and fast to the idealism for which the Little Theatre was founded. Having done magnificently in Cape Cod they moved over to MacDougal Street, New York, and continued to do wonders artistically under Cook's leadership. It was here, one may say, that Eugene O'Neill was born into the world of art and drama, and had the Provincetown Players not given him his chance he might not have attained the fame he now enjoys.

These Players also brought to light the now famous Susan Gaspell as a playwright, and the now eminent scenic artists, Robert Edmund Jones and Norman Bel-Geddes.

Some of the players began to look longingly towards the bright lights of Broadway's theatrical district, the Mecca of all actors, and no doubt in fancy saw their names blazoned forth in electric light over the entrance of some commercial theatre. Their ideals slowly vanished when they began to rub elbows with commerce. George Cam Cook, seeing the tide of affairs, quietly took his leave of " The Provincetown Players."

The good ship Idealism that Cook had steered smoothly and merrily for so long felt his departure like any human thing, and grounded on the golden rocks of commercialism, sinking with all hands on deck, never to rise again—thus proving that Gold and Idealism do not sail smoothly side by side.

Over on the East Side of New York a third group came into existence under the name of "The Neighbourhood Players," and under the guidance of the Seligman sisters.

This Litttle Theatre group did splendid work and made history with two outstanding productions: *The Dybbuk*, by Eugene O'Neill, and *The Little Clay Cart*, by King Sudraka, a Jewish author.

Out in the western cities there arose "The Chicago Art Theatre" in Chicago, the Arts and Crafts Theatre in Detroit, Michigan, and the Indianapolis Little Theatre in Indianapolis.

At the University of Toronto, Canada, there was established "The Hart House Theatre," one of the finest of its kind on the American continent, and now world-renowned.

In more recent years, Miss Eva Le-Gallienne became instrumental in founding, outside New York's regular theatrical district, The Repertory Theatre, which in these few short years has become the miracle theatre of the city. This theatre, standing far away from the heart of Broadway, has earned a reputation for magnificent productions of beauty and decency for which one must be sincerely thankful in these days of demoralization in the commercial theatre.

The Irish Guild of Players are now established at The American Laboratory Theatre, 222 East 54th Street, and an Irish Theatre in New York seems to have become a definite institution. They are now playing *Family Failings*, by William Boyle. The organization is in its second successful year.

Brooklyn, New York, has a beautiful Little Theatre, and some splendid plays are to be seen there. The players are both professional and amateur.

Over in Philadelphia there is the Duse Art Theatre, founded in 1925, which gives some artistic productions of old and new plays.

The Universities of America are now famous for their magnificent theatres.

Princetown University received a gift of two hundred and fifty thousand dollars to build a theatre.

The Carnegie Institute has a Little Theatre famous under the direction of Ben Iden Payne, one-time manager at the Abbey, Dublin.

A glance at the list of Little Theatres will give the reader some idea of the number in the United States.

For the past seven years a Little Theatre Tournament has been held in New York for the David Bellasco Prize Cup, and groups of players come from many countries to compete. The cup was won for the year 1929 by the Garden Players of Forest Hill Gardens, L.I., who presented Sir James Barrie's *Shall We Join the Ladies?*

Many magazines are devoted to Little Theatre work, the most notable being the "Theatre Arts Monthly," "The Drama," "The Little Theatre Monthly," "The Little Theatre News." and "The Billboard's Little Theatre Handbook." The latter is published by The Billboard Publishing Company, to whom I am indebted for the following partial list of Little Theatres in America.

Representative Little Theatres of America which have sprung from the Abbey.

ALABAMA.

AUBURN.—*Auburn Players.* Prof. Harry L. Hamilton, director.
BIRMINGHAM.—*Little Theatre of Birmingham,* 2144 Highland Avenue. Bernard Szold, director.
MOBILE.—*Little Theatre of Mobile,* 65 Church Street (Box 114)
SELMA.—*Selma Drama League Players.*

ALASKA.

KETCHIKAN.—*Ketchikan High School Players.* Emery F. ¡Tobin, director.

ARIZONA.

PHŒNIX.—*Little Theatre,* 100 McDowell Road.
PHŒNIX.—*Arizona Play Actors,* 1208 Eastmoreland. Walter Ben Hare, director.
TUCSON.—*University Epworth League.* Betty McVey, director.

ARKANSAS.

MORRILLTON.—*Harding Dramatic Club of Harding College.*

CALIFORNIA.

ALHAMBRA.—*Alhambra San Gabriel Community Players,* 104 E. Main Street. Richard Sterling, director.
BERKELEY.—*Campus Little Theatre.*
BERKELEY.—*University of California Little Theatre.*
CARMEL-BY-THE-SEA.—*Little Theatre Arts and Crafts Club.*
FRUITVALE.—*The St. Elizabeth Players,* 1530 34th Avenue.
GLENDALE.—*Community Players* (The Littlest Theatre), 620 E. Broadway. Harold Brewster, director.
HOLLYWOOD.—*The Writers' Club,* 6700 Sunset Boulevard. Arthur Lubin, secretary.
HOLLYWOOD.—*Art Theatre of Hollywood,* 602 S. Alvarado Street. Dr. T. Percival Gerson, secretary.
LAKEPORT.—*Little Theatre Co.* Berkely Haswell, director.
LONG BEACH.—*Little Art Theatre,* Chamber of Commerce.
LONG BEACH.—*Community Players,* Community Hall, 9th and Lime Streets. Jack H. Sterling, director.
LONG BEACH.—*Bohemian Arts Theatre,* 3102 Anaheim Street. Revan D'Arcy Komaroff, director.

LOS ANGELES.—*Garret Club,* 132½ S. Spring Street. Charles Moore, director.

LOS ANGELES.—*Literary Theatre of Los Angeles,* Gamut Club Building, 1044 S. Hope Street. Frayne Williams, director.

LOS ANGELES.—*Los Angeles Opera and Fine Arts Club,* 1131 Elden Street. Mrs. J. T. Anderson, president.

LOS ANGELES.—*Potboiler Art Theatre,* Gamut Club Building, 1044 S. Hope Street. Ole M. Ness, director.

LOS ANGELES.—*Los Angeles Theatre Guild,* 315 N. Hancock Street. Frank Cantello, Secretary.

LOS ANGELES.—*Venice Community Players.* Ursula March Largey, director.

OAKLAND.—*University of California Little Theatre.*

PASADENA.—*Community Playhouse Association,* 39 S. El Molina Avenue. Gilmor Brown, director.

PASADENA.—*English Club of California Institute of Technology,* Culbertson Hall. G. R. MacMinn, director.

PASADENA.—*Young People's Dramatic Club.*

POMONA.—*Ganesha Players,* 146 E. Third Street. Smith Russell, secretary.

REDLANDS.—*Redlands Community Players.*

SAN FRANCISCO.—*Players' Guild Theatre,* 1757 Bush Street. Reginald Travers, director.

SAN JOSE.—*DeMolay Players,* 148 N. Third Street. C. C. Clark, secretary.

SAN FRANCISCO.—*Community Players of the Y. M. Y. W. H. A.,* 121 Haight Street. Mrs. Louis H. Blumenthal, business manager.

SAN DIEGO.—*San Diego Players,* Yorick Theatre. Francis P. Buckley, director.

SANTA BARBARA.—*Community Arts Players,* Lobero Theatre. Irving Pichel, director.

SANTA ANA.—*Santa Ana Players.*

SANTA MONICA.—*Dramatic Club, Santa Monica Bay Women's Clubs,* 1210 Fourth Street.

STOCKTON.—*Pacific Players,* College of the Pacific. De Marcus Brown, director.

WHITTIER.—*Community Players,* care of Y.M.C.A., Miss Marian H. Weed, Secretary.

COLORADO.

BOULDER.—*University of Colorado Little Theatre,* 1220 Grand View. G. F. Reynolds, director.

COLORADO SPRINGS.—*Colorado Springs Drama League.*

DENVER.—*Community Players.* E. B. Sargent, director.

DENVER.—*South High Dramatic Club,* South Pearl and Colorado Avenues. Christine C. Buck, secretary.

CONNECTICUT.

BRIDGEPORT.—*New Century Players,* 1074 Iranistan Avenue. Grace D. Clarke, director.

BRIDGEPORT.—*Little Theatre League,* 25 Laurel Avenue. Julia Farnam, secretary.

BRIDGEPORT.—*Senior Student Players.* Grace Dalrymple Clark, director.

BRISTOL.—*Little Theatre,* Memorial High School. R. S. Newell, director.

BRISTOL.—*Bristol Community Players,* 249 Main Street.

GLASTONBURY.—*Williams Memorial Hall,* Main Street. W. R. Campbell, director.

HARTFORD.—*Little Theatre Guild of Hartford,* 55 Sterling Street. Esther Gross, secretary.

HARTFORD.—*Hartford Women's Club.*

LITCHFIELD.—*The Litchfield Players.* Miss Inga Westerburg, Secretary.

MADISON.—*Jitney Players,* Inc., Little Red House, Boston Post Road. Bushnell Cheney, director.

NEW HAVEN.—*The Playcraftsmen of Yale University,* 1847 Yale Station. Richard C. Lowesburg, secretary.

NEW MILFORD.—*Haybarn Theatre,* Western View Farm.

NORWALK.—*Silvermine Guild,* Silvermine. Marguerite Hamilton, director.

STAMFORD.—*Onax Dramatic Players.*

WESTPORT.—*Little Theatre Players.* Charles Fable, treasurer.

DELAWARE.

NEWARK.—*Women's College Dramatic Club,* Wolf Hall.

WILMINGTON.—*Air Castle Players,* Victoria Hortz, secretary.

WILMINGTON.—*Wilmington Drama League.*

DISTRICT OF COLUMBIA.

WASHINGTON.—*The Arts Club.*

WASHINGTON.—*Ram Head Players,* Wardman Park Inn.

WASHINGTON.—*The Departmental Players,* 2209 Eye Street, N.W. John J. Campbell, business manager.

WASHINGTON.—*Lenore Marie DeGrange Children Players,* 1756 Kilbourne Place, N.W.

WASHINGTON.—*The Little Negro Theatre.*

WASHINGTON.—*The Krigwa Players.*

FLORIDA.

DELAND.—*Green Room Players,* Stetson University. Irving C. Stover, director.

JACKSONVILLE.—*Jacksonville Community Players.*

MIAMI.—*Little Theatre, Miami University.* Howard Southgate, director.

MIAMI.—*Miami Civic Theatre,* care Mrs. Addison Hall, Miami " Daily News."

PALATKA.—*Palatka Community Service.*

PENSACOLA.—*Little Theatre,* 24 E. Romana Street. B. W. Sims, director.

TAMPA.—*Community Players,* 2810 Jefferson. Earl Stumpf, director.

WINTER PARK.—*Rollins College Players of Little Theatre Workshop.* Orpha Pope Grey, director.

GEORGIA.

ATLANTA.—*Playcrafters.*

AUGUSTA.—*Little Theatre League,* 305 Montgomery Building. Agnes Brewer, director.

ATLANTA.—*Oglethorpe University Players Theatre.* Lewis Haase, director.

COLUMBUS.—*Little Theatre League,* Court House, Department of Recreation. Walter J. Cartier, director.

SAVANNAH.—*Town Theatre.* Spencer P. Henley, president.

ILLINOIS.

BLOOMINGTON.—*Bloomington Community Players.* Ethel Gunn, secretary.

CENTRALIA.—*Little Egyptian Theatre,* Board of Recreation. Eddie Walkup, director.

CHAMPAIGN.—*Illinois Theatre Guild,* Ill. Union Building, Paul Wilson, director.

CHICAGO.—*Duo-Masque Players,* 59 East Grand Avenue.

CHICAGO.—*Chicago Play Producing Co.,* 360 N. Michigan Blvd.

CHICAGO.—*Temple Players,* Temple Judea. Walter A. Lyons, director.

CHICAGO.—*College Players,* 822 Buena Avenue. Fritz Blocki, secretary.

CHICAGO.—*Studio Players,* 826 N. Clark Street. Phyllis Udell, director.

CHICAGO.—*The Art Club,* care Mrs. John A. Carpenter, 710 Rush Street.

CHICAGO.—*The Boys' Dramatic Club,* care Bertha Iles, director, 430 Fine Arts Building.

CHICAGO.—*Coffer-Miller Players,* 631 Fine Arts Building, 410 S. Michigan Boulevard.
CHICAGO.—*Children's Civic Theatre of Chicago,* 410 S. Michigan Avenue. Bertha L. Iles, director.
CHICAGO.—*Rosary College Dramatic Club,* 5454 Everett Avenue. Mildred North, secretary.
CHICAGO.—*Æthiops Little Theatre* (Coloured) School, 419 E. 50th Street. Alfred M. Ligon, Managing director.
CHICAGO.—*Grace Hickox Studio Players,* Fine Arts Building.
CHICAGO.—*Drama League of America,* 59 E. Van Buren Street. George Junkin, field secretary.
CHICAGO.—*Hull House Players,* Hull House Theatre, 800 Halsted Street. Maurice J. Cooney.
CHICAGO.—*Dramatic Department, Chemical National Bank of N. Y.,* 230 S. Clark Street.
CHICAGO.—*Dramatic Department, American Woollen Co. of N. Y.,* 223 W. Jackson Boulevard.
CHICAGO.—*Little Theatre,* 4800 Lake Park Avenue.
CHICAGO.—*Players' Club, Jewish People's Institute,* 1258 Taylor Avenue. Lester Alden, director.
CHICAGO.—*Playcraft Theatre,* 867 N. Dearborn Street. H. W. Keedy, director.
CHICAGO.—*Sinai Players.* Emil G. Hirsch, director.
CHICAGO.—*Shadows Art Theatre.* Broadcasting Station, WHT.
DECATUR.—*Decatur Little Theatre.*
EVANSTON.—*Campus Players,* North Western University. Alexander Dean, secretary.
GALESBURG.—*Knox College.* C. L. Menser, secretary.
LAKE FOREST.—*Garrick Players,* Lake Forest College.
PEORIA.—*Players' Club,* 601 State Street. W. F. Hertel, secretary.
PEORIA.—*Peoria Players,* 211 N. Monroe Street. Miss E. A. Pulsipher, secretary.
SPRINGFIELD.—*Community Players* 725 S. 7th Street. Henry House, secretary.
WOODSTOCK.—*Paint and Powder Club.* Helen Sandford, director.

INDIANA.

EVANSVILLE.—*Drama League,* 49 Washington Avenue. Clara Vickery, secretary.
FRENCH LICK.—*French Lick Players.* Laurence R. Taylor, director.
GARY.—*Gary Musical Academy,* 539 Broadway.
INDIANAPOLIS.—*Little Theatre Society of Indianapolis,* 126 E. 14th Street. Lillian F. Hamilton, Exec. Secretary.
INDIANAPOLIS.—*Little Theatre Society,* care Clarence M. Weesner, the John Herron Art Institute.
INDIANAPOLIS.—*Little Theatre Society,* care Mrs. William O. Bates, 756 Middle Drive.

INDIANAPOLIS.—*Indianapolis Theatre Guild,* Inc., Room 218
5 E. Market Street.
INDIANAPOLIS.—*The Players,* Indiana College of Music and
Fine Arts.

IOWA.

AMES.—*Masque Players,* State College, Box 425 Sta. A.
Nancy E. Eilcot, secretary.
CEDAR RAPIDS.—*Coe College Little Theatre.*
COUNCIL BLUFFS.—*Attic Studios Theatre,* Bennett Building.
DES MOINES.—*Community Drama Association,* Drake University. Frances Herriott, director.
DES MOINES.—*Gilpin Players,* 704 Insurance Exchange Building, Sylpha Snook, director.
DUBUQUE.—*Towne Players.* Bill Voights, business manager.
DUBUQUE.—*St. John Players,* 13th and White Streets. Frances
Miller, Secretary.
GRINNELL.—*Play Production Class,* Grinnell College. W. H.
Trumbauer, director.
IOWA CITY.—*The University Theatre,* University of Iowa, Hall
of Natural Science. Miss Dorothy McCleuelian, secretary.
KNOXVILLE.—*Knoxville Players.* Carl Cook Macy.
MASON CITY.—*Drama Shop Players,* 229 Second Street, N.E.
F. K. Tressel, Secretary.
MYSTIC.—*Mystic Dramatic Club.* Paul E. Hunter, secretary.
NEWTON.—*Little Theatre Association,* 709 N. Second Avenue,
E. N. R. Moore.
PRAIRIE CITY.—*Prairie City Community Players.* W. S. Parker,
manager.

KANSAS.

LAWRENCE.—*University of Kansas Little Theatre.*
MANHATTAN.—*Purple Masque Players,* State Agricultural
College. H. Miles Heberer, director.
OTTAWA.—*Ottawa University Players' Club.* Naomi Wenzelmann, director.
PITTSBURG.—*Theta Alpha Phi,* State Teachers' College. Prof.
J. R. Pelsma, director.

KENTUCKY.

BARBOURVILLE.—*National Theatre.* J. L. Hoffin, secretary.
LEXINGTON.—*Campus Playhouse.* University of Kentucky,
Box 545. Prof. W. R. Sutherland, director.
LOUISVILLE.—*Y. M. H. A. Players.* Second and Jacob Streets.
Louis M. Roth, president.
LOUISVILLE.—*The University Players, The Playhouse.* Boyd
Martin, director.

LOUISVILLE.—*Trinity Council, Y. M. I. Dramatic Club,* Baxter and Morton Avenues. Arch. J. Curran, director.
LOUISVILLE.—*The Playhouse,* University of Louisville.
LOUISVILLE.—*Dramatic Committee, Knights of Columbus.*

LOUISIANA.

BATON ROUGE.—*Little Theatre Guild,* 140 St. Joseph Street. Mrs. H. K. Strickland, president.
MORGAN CITY.—*Teche Players,* 508 Everett Street.   Frank L. Prohaska, secretary.
NEW ORLEANS.—*Dramatic Club,* Tulane University.
NEW ORLEANS.—*Dramatic Class of the New Orleans Conservatory of Music and Dramatic Art.*
NEW ORLEANS.—*Dramatic Society, Young Women's Hebrew Association.*
NEW ORLEANS.—*Jefferson College Players.*
NEW ORLEANS.—*Le Petit Theatre du Vieux Carre.* 530 St. Peter Street.   Bennett Kilpack, director.
NEW ORLEANS.—*Philo Society.* Rabbi Raphael Gold, director.
NEW ORLEANS.—*Players' Guild,* Menorah Institute, Euterpe Street, near St. Charles Avenue.
SHREVEPORT.—*Shreveport Little Theatre.*   Arthur Maitland, director.

MAINE.

ELIOT.—*Green Acre Theatre Guild Little Theatre.*
LEWISTON.—*The English 4 A Players,* Bates College.   Att. Prof. A. Craig Baird.

MARYLAND.

BALTIMORE.—*Homewood Players,* John Hopkin's University.
BALTIMORE.—*Baltimore Children's Theatre,* Lyric Theatre, Mount Royal Avenue.   Frederick R. Huber, secretary.
BALTIMORE.—*Vagabond Players.*
BALTIMORE.—*All University Dramatic Club,* John Hopkin's University.   Albert G. Langehittig, jun., secretary.
BALTIMORE.—*The Play Arts Guild,* Inc., s.w. cor. Morton and 23rd Streets.   John W. Cushing, president.
BRUNSWICK.—*Dramatic Club.*   Marjorie Leslie, director.
FROSTBURG.—*State Normal School,* Loo Street.   Thelma Harvey, secretary.

MASSACHUSETTS.

AMHERST.—*Roister Dramatic Society,* 88 Pleasant Street. Edward F. Ingraham, secretary.
BOSTON.—*Theatre Guild of Boston,* 417 Pierce Building. John Gutterson, secretary.

BOSTON.—*Children's Theatre,* care Emerson College of Oratory.

BOSTON.—*Waban Neighbourhood Club.* Harry L. Tilton, manager.

BOSTON.—*The Outdoor Players,* Pierce Building.

BOSTON.—*Little Theatre Players,* 89 Gainsboro Street. Victoria Covington, secretary.

BOSTON.—*Actors' Play Shop,* 89 Gainsboro Street. Raymond Gilbert, director.

BOSTON.—*Boston Stage Society,* The Barn Theatre, 36 Joy Street.

BOSTON.—*Towne Studio of Dramatic Art,* 6 Byron Street, Hugh William Towne, director.

CAMBRIDGE.—*Larchwood Players,* Bungalow Theatre, Larch Road.

DEERFIELD.—*Dramatic Society of Deerfield Academy.*

FRAMINGHAM.—*The Wardrobe Club.* Mrs. C. Fuller, 31 Warren Road.

GLOUCESTER.—*School of Little Theatre,* Rocky Neck Street. Stuart Guthrie secretary.

HOLYOKE.—*English* 26 *Playshop,* Mount Holyoke College, Chapin Auditorium.

LEOMINSTER.—*Community Players.* Nell Kimball, president.

LAWRENCE.—*St. John Dramatic Society,* P. O. Box 22. W. Ridings, secretary.

NEW BEDFORD.—*The Camphor Players' Studio,* 86 Court Street. Mr. McEwen, director.

NEW BEDFORD.—*Student Players,* 104 South Street. Rebecca Berkowitz, director.

NORTHAMPTON.—*Senior Dramatic Society,* Smith College.

OAK BLUFFS.—*Martha's Vineyard—Phidelah Rice Players.*

PITTSFIELD.—*Town Players of Pittsfield.* Miss Selina Mace, director.

PROVINCETOWN.—*Wharf Players.*

PROVINCETOWN.—*Winston-Moore Players.*

PROVINCETOWN.—*Harry Kemp Players.*

PROVINCETOWN.—*Barnstormers' Theatre.* I. Merril, business manager.

SOUTH MIDDLEBORO.—*The Cape Players.* Henry B. Burkland.

SPRINGFIELD.—*Unity Players.* Mrs. H. L. Sullivan, director.

TUFT'S COLLEGE.—*Pen, Paint, and Pretzels Dramatic Society of Tuft's College.*

WABAN.—*Waban Neighbourhood Club,* Beacon Street. George N. Roberts, director.

WILLIAMSTOWN.—*Williams Little Theatre,* Jesup Hall. Hugh Murdoch MacMullan, director.

WILLIAMSTOWN.—*Cap and Bells,* Inc., Robert W. Post, secretary.

MICHIGAN.

BIRMINGHAM.—*Village Players of Birmingham.* P. O. Box 201.

BLOOMINGDALE.—*Little Theatre.* Mrs. E. A. Carnes, director.

DETROIT.—*Dramatic Class of Northeastern H. S.* Joseph Weslosky, secretary.

DETROIT.—*Theatre Association of Detroit,* 10620 Foley Avenue. Albert Riebling, director.

DETROIT.—*Detroit New Century Club.* Harriette G. Locke, chairman.

DETROIT.—*Temple Beth El Arts Society.* Frank V. Martin, secretary.

DETROIT.—*Theatre Arts Club,* 711 Lake Shore Road. Mrs. G. W. Zangu, secretary.

DETROIT.—*The Nor.-E. Players.* John Francis Carrica, managing director.

DETROIT.—*Detroit Repertory Theatre,* 52 Putnam Street.

HILLSDALE.—*Department of Dramatic Art,* Hillsdale College. Professor Sawyer Falk.

MONROE.—*Community Players,* Community Service. Mrs. Peter F. Stair, director; H. D. Schubert, exec. director.

PETERSBURG.—*Little Theatre.* Lillian Mortimer, director.

PONTIAC.—*Pontiac Little Theatre.*

SAGINAW.—*Little Theatre,* Hoyt Library Building. Harry G. Miller, secretary.

YPSILANTI.—*Ypsilanti Players,* 133 Rear North Huron Street.

MINNESOTA.

DULUTH.—*Duluth College Club and A. A. U. W.* Mrs. S. Shepard, director.

DULUTH.—*Little Theatre of Duluth,* Inc., F. C. Tenny, secretary, 415 Board of Trade Building.

MINNEAPOLIS.—*Portal Playhouse Players,* 3437 Stevens Avenue, Apt. 7. Dean Jenson.

MINNEAPOLIS.—*MacPhail Little Theatre Co.,* Lasalle at 15th. Jack DeVere.

MINNEAPOLIS.—*St. Stephen's Players,* 1819 Lyndale Avenue, South Suite 222. A. H. Faust, director.

MINNEAPOLIS.—*Univ. Dramatic Club,* Univ. of Minneapolis, 18 Music Bldg. A. M. Dingwall, secretary.

MINNEAPOLIS.—*Studio Players,* 624 New York Life Building.

MINNEAPOLIS.—*Lawry Day Producing Productions,* 1012 E. 18th Street.

MINNEAPOLIS.—*Jordan Community Players.* Alyce L. Smith, secretary.

MONTEVIDEO.—*Montevideo Dramatic Club.* Agnes E. Holstad, secretary.

NORTHFIELD.—*Grand Theatre,* cor. Washington and Second Streets. Ervel Disley, director.

VIRGINIA.—*Virgina Junior College,* High School Auditorium. Esther R. Sprester, director.

MISSISSIPPI.

McCOMB.—*Little Theatre.* Mrs. A. K. Landau, president.

TOUGALOO.—*Robeson Dramatic Club,* Tougaloo College, Lilian W. Voorhees, director.

MISSOURI.

BOONVILLE.—*Kemper Dramatic Club,* Kemper Military School.

COLUMBIA.—*Missouri Workshop,* University of Mo. Jesse Hall, director, Room 116.

KANSAS CITY.—*Theatre Craft Guild.*

KANSAS CITY.—*Chanticleer Players.*

KANSAS CITY.—*Kansas City Theatre,* 600 Altman Building. L. Logan Smith, director-manager.

SPRINGFIELD.—*The Pill Box Little Theatre,* 874 Boulevard. Floyd C. Mosely.

ST. LOUIS.—*Neighbourhood House Players,* 19th and Washington Streets. George Junkin, director.

ST. LOUIS.—*New Toy Theatre,* 457 N. Boyle Avenue. Elizabeth More, general manager.

ST. LOUIS.—*Devereux Players,* Artists' Guild, 810 N. Union building.

MONTANA.

BOZEMAN.—*Bozeman's Woman's Club,* 605 S. 6th Street. Mrs. F. 1. Powers, secretary.

DILLON.—*The Gargoyles,* State Normal College. Mary K. Sands, director.

MISSOULA.—*Missoula University Masquers.*

RED LODGE.—*Mask and Frolic Club.*

NEBRASKA.

LINCOLN.—*Carroll's Little Theatre,* Nebraska State Bank Building. Harvey H. Carroll, director.

OMAHA.—*The Community Players.* Alan McDonald, president.

YORK.—*College Auditorum Players.*

NEW HAMPSHIRE.

HANOVER.—*Dartmouth Players.*
PETERBORO.—*Outdoor Players.* Marie W. Laughton, director.

NEW JERSEY.

ATLANTIC CITY.—*Boardwalk Players,* Steeplechase Pier Park. George V. Hobart, director.
BAYONNE.—*Bayonne Theatre Guild.* Thomas J. Gormley, secretary, 42 W. 50th Street.
BOGOTA.—*Footlights Club,* 136 Larch Avenue. Dean H. Eadie, director.
EAST ORANGE.—*College Club of the Oranges,* Church House. Mrs. Charles E. Dull, director.
HIGHTSTOWN.—*Hightstown Players,* Wilson Hall. G. W. Marque Maier, secretary.
JERSEY CITY.—*Palisade Players.* Julia Brown, director.
JERSEY CITY.—*Playfair Players,* care Royal Hinrichs, 20 Lexington Avenue.
JERSEY CITY.—*Jersey Playmakers,* care Howard T. Lakey, 36 Rutgers Avenue.
JERSEY CITY.—*Minerva Club,* care Y. W. C. A., 43 Belmont Avenue.
MADISON.—*Green Door Players,* Madison Settlement, Cook Avenue. Ernest H. Smith, secretary.
NEWARK.—*The Thalians,* Barringer High School. Franklin Crosse, secretary.
PLAINFIELD.—*Plainfield Community Players.*
PRINCETON.—*Princeton Theatre Intime.* R. McClenahan, secretary.
RIVERTON.—*Acorn Players.*
SUMMIT.—*The Playhouse Association,* Tulip Street. Norman Lee Swartout, director.
TRENTON.—*Trenton Group Players.*
WESTFIELD.—*Mask and Mime Club.*

NEW MEXICO.

SANTA FE.—*Santa Fe Community Players.*

NEW YORK.

ALBANY.—*St. Patrick's Players,* Central and Lake Avenues.
ALLEGANY.—*Bonaventure Players,* St. Bonaventure's College. Professor Joseph Yanner, M.A., director.
ASTORIA, L. I.—*Precious Blood Players,* 393 Broadway. D. F. Barreca, secretary.

Appendix B 185

AUBURN.—*Auburn Amateur Dramatic Club.*

BATAVIA.—*Crosby Players,* Denio Apartments.   Harry D. Crosby, secretary.

BAY RIDGE.—*Ovington Players,* Bay Ridge High School.

BROOKLYN.—*Brooklyn Heights Players,* 104 Clark Street.

BROOKLYN.—*The Troupers,* St. Francis College, 41 Butler Street.

BROOKLYN.—*Neighbourhood Drama Guild of Beechview,* 1738 W. 12th Street.   Lya Margulies, secretary.

BROOKLYN.—*Brooklyn Players,* 1721 E. 22nd Street.

BROOKLYN.—*Mission Relief Players,* 45 Foxall Street. Joseph P. Bretano.

BROOKLYN.—*Little Theatre Committee,* 126 St. Felix Street. Judge F. E. Crane, secretary.

BROOKLYN.—*Institute Players,* 30 Lafayette Avenue. Charles D. Atkins, secretary.

BROOKLYN.—*Bensonhurst Theatre Guild,* 60 Bay 31st Street, Bernard Katz, director.

BROOKLYN.—*Clark Street Players.*

BROOKLYN.—*Shaw Players,* 120 Jackson Street.   Joseph Bascetta, president.

BROOKLYN.—*The MacLaughlin Players,* 419 Flushing Avenue, Jo Abramson, secretary.

BROOKLYN.—*Acme Players,* Acme Hall, 7th Avenue and 9th Street.

BROOKLYN.—*The Thespians,* 149 Amherst Street.   Herbert G. Bliven, secretary.

BROOKLYN.—*Court Players,* 1728 Madison Street.   W. B. Kasparoit.

BROOKLYN.—*Old Fort Club,* 50 Monroe Place.   Charles S. Soule, director.

BROOKLYN.—*Radio Theatre Players,* 211 Bay 7th Street. Alfred L. Rigali, director.

BROOKLYN.—*Plymouth Players,* Plymouth Church.   Beatrice Beecher, director.

BROOKLYN.—*Lew Dick Players,* 217 Bristol Street.

BROOKLYN.—*Talisman Troupe,* 126 St. Felix Street.   Jane Kerley, director.

BROOKLYN.—*International Theatre Arts Institute,* 102 Remsen Street.   Mr. Mussey, director.

BUFFALO.—*Dramatic Society of the Cansisius College.*

BUFFALO.—*Buffalo Players,* Inc., 545 Elmwood Avenue. Harold P. Preston, director.

BUFFALO.—*D'Youville Players.*

BUFFALO.—*Two-in-One Players of Buffalo,* 1589 Broadway. Ed. Sommer.

DUNKIRK.—*Dunkirk Players.*   Edward C. Kraus, director.

ELMHURST, L. I.—*Elmhurst Jackson Heights Players.*

ELMIRA.—*Elmira Community Service,* 413 E. Water Street. Z. Nesbor, secretary.

FLATBUS.—*Neighbourhood Playhouse,* 2238-2240 Church Av.
FLUSHING, L. I.—*League Players,* League Buildings.   Sarah
C. Palime, secretary.
FOREST HILLS, L. I.—*Garden Players,* 11 Greenway Terrace.
Helen Hoeft, secretary.
FREDONIA.—*Dramatic Club of Normal School,* Normal Audit-
orium.
GENEVA.—*Medbery Mummers,* Hobart College. Mrs. Murray
Bartlett and Prof. John Muirheid, directors.
GLEN MORRIS.—*Richmond Hill South Dramatic Society,* 10772
111th Street.   Ed. Mackert.
GOUVERNEUR.—*Gouveneur Players,* care Howard Collins.
HARTSDALE.—*Wayside Players.*
ITHACA.—*Cornell Dramatic Club,* Goldwin Smith Hall.   Le
Verne Baldwin, secretary.
ITHACA.—*Ithaca Conservatory of Music,* Williams School of
Expression and Dramatic Art.
MAMARONECK.—*Mamaroneck Community Players.*
MOUNT KISCO.—*Northern Westchester Players.*
MOUNT VERNON.—*Mount Vernon Community Players,* 48 S.
Second Avenue.   R. M. Rogers, president.
NEW ROCHELLE.—*Huguenot Players.*   Miss B. Lowenthal,
secretary, 153 Elm Street.
NEW YORK.—*Laboratory Players* of University Extension,
Columbia University, 140 Claremont Avenue. Mrs. Estelle H.
Davis, director.
NEW YORK.—*Philolexian Soc.* of Columbia College, Columbia
University.
NEW YORK.—*"Wigs and Cues"* of Barnard College, Columbia
University.
NEW YORK.—*Sophomore Class Show* of Columbia College,
Columbia University.
NEW YORK.—*Varsity Show of Columbia College,* Columbia
University.
NEW YORK.—*The Performers,* 248 E. 80th Street.   Murray
Weir, director.
NEW YORK.—*Meeting House Theatre,* 550 W. 110th Street.
Fay Baker, director.
NEW YORK.—*Labour Temperance Players,* care Labour Temple
School, 239 E. 14th Street.
NEW YORK.—*Bramhall Players,* 138 E. 27th Street.   Butler
Davenport, director.
NEW YORK.—*Curtain Players,* 12 W. 76th Street.   Richard A.
Zinn, director.
NEW YORK.—*Children's Dramatic League,* Hotel Astor. Elsie
Oppenheim, secretary.
NEW YORK.—*Civic Club,* Drama Group, 14 W. 12th Street.
NEW YORK.—*Dramatic Department, Community Service,* 315
Fourth Avenue.   George Junkin, secretary.

NEW YORK.—*Children's Theatre,* Fifth Avenue and 104th Street. Clare T. Major, secretary.

NEW YORK.—*Inter-Theatre Arts,* Inc., 42 Commerce Street.

NEW YORK.—*" The Snarks,"* care The N. Y. Comedy Club, 240 East 68th Street. Mrs. Danforth.

NEW YORK.—*Washington Square College Players,* 100 Washington Square. Thomas H. Mullen.

NEW YORK.—*The Senior Players,* Evander Childs High School, 184th Street, and Creston Avenue.

NEW YORK.—*Marionette Theatre Studio,* 27 W. 8th Street. Florence Koeller, secretary.

NEW YORK CITY.—*Cooper Players* of Cooper Union Institute.

NEW YORK.—*Lenox Hill Players,* 248 W. 14th Street.

NEW YORK.—*The Drama House,* 108 W. 59th Street. William H. Bridge, director.

NEW YORK.—*The Triangle,* 7th Avenue and 11th Street.

NEW YORK CITY.—*Guild Players, University Settlement,* 184 Eldridge Street.

NEW YORK CITY.—*Hunter College " The Pipers."*

NEW YORK.—*Poet's Theatre,* 28 E. 10th Street. Harry Kemp, director.

NEW YORK.—*Kittridge Players,* 440 E. 57th Street.

NEW YORK.—*Washington Heights Players,* 209 Duckman Street. Marita Rosler, director.

NEW YORK.—*Professional Woman's Little Theatre Co.,* care Professional Woman's League, 56 West 53rd Street. Ullie Akerstrom, director.

NEW YORK.—*Strolling Players,* 1121 West Farms Road. Mabel De Vries, secretary.

NEW YORK.—*School of the Theatre,* 571 Lexington Avenue.

NEW YORK.—*Irvine Players,* 31 Riverside Drive. Miss Theodora U. Irvine, director.

NEW YORK.—*The Frogs,* Inc. (Negros), 46 W. 135th Street.

NEW YORK.—*The Mimers,* 137 W. 38th Street. Edward Sargent Brown, director.

NEW YORK.—*Vagabond Players,* 137 W. 38th Street.

NEW YORK.—*Cherry Lane Players,* 40 Commerce Street. William S. Rainey, director.

NEW YORK.—*Lighthouse Players,* 111 E. 59th Street. Rosalie Mathieu, director.

NEW YORK.—*Young People's Organization* of St. Paul's Church, 86th Street and West End Avenue. Miss Aida Gordon, director.

NEW YORK.—*Greenwich House Players,* 27 Barrow Street.

NEW YORK.—*The Schiff Centre Players.* Jacob H. Schiff Centre, 2510 Valentine Avenue, Bronx, New York.

NEW YORK.—*Henry Players,* Henry Street Settlement, 301 Henry Street.

NEW YORK.—*Stockbridge Stocks,* 79 Seventh Avenue.

NEW YORK.—*Vassar Philaletheis Association,* Vassar College. Eliz. H. Fenner, public manager.

NEW YORK.—*Lyceum Theatre, American Academy of Dramatic Art,* West 45th Street, near Broadway.

NEW YORK.—*Cellar Players,* 436 W. 27th Street. Adele Gutman Nathan, director.

NEW YORK.—*Association Players, Y. M. H. A.,* 92nd Street. Myron E. Sattler, director.

NEW YORK.—*Junior Performers,* 714 W. 181 Street. Helen M. Fox, director.

NEW YORK.—*Amateur Comedy Club,* Inc., 150 E. 36th Street.

NEW YORK.—*Chrystie Little Theatre Guild,* Recreation Room and Settlement, 186 Chrystie Street. Lee Strasberg, director.

NEW YORK.—*The Harlequinaders,* 40 E. 35th Street.

NEW YORK.—*The Players Guild,* Dramatic Department of Washington Heights, Y. M. H. A., 159th Street, and St. Nicholas Avenue. Myron Sattler, director.

NEW YORK.—*S. A. J.,* 15 W. 86th Street. Myron Sattler, director.

NEW YORK.—*Monticello Players,* 237 E. 104th Street.

NIAGARA FALLS.—*The Players of Niagara.*

NYACK.—*Nyack Players.*

OSSINING.—*Ossining Players,* 6 N. Malcolm Street.

PELHAM MANOR.—*Playshop Players.*

PELHAM MANOR.—*Manor Club Players.,* H. E. Dey, secretary.

PLEASANTVILLE.—*Pleasantville Players.*

PORT CHESTER.—*Port Chester Players.*

POUGHKEEPSIE.—*Outdoor Theatre,* Vassar College.

POUGHKEEPSIE.— *Poughkeepsie Community Theatre.*

ROCHESTER.—*Laboratory of Theatre Arts,* 134 South Avenue.

ROCHESTER (Argyle Street).—*Prince Street Players.*

ROCHESTER.—*The Make-Up Box Theatre,* 218 East Avenue. Ned Hungerford, director.

ROCHESTER.—*The Towne Players,* 186 East Avenue.

ROCHESTER.—*Community Players,* Clinton Avenue at Meigs Street, 2nd Baptist Church.

ROCKVILLE CENTRE, L. I.—*Institute Players.*

ROCKVILLE CENTRE.—*Fortnightly Club.* Edna Hutchins, secretary.

RYE.—*Rye Community Players.*

SCARBORO-ON-HUDSON.—*Beechwood Players.* Miss Marian Dinwiddle, ex-secretary.

SCHENECTADY.—*Sphinx Players,* 1029 State Street. Raymond P. Ham, business manager.

SCHENECTADY.—*The Harlequinaders.* John Loftus, secretary, 209 Nott Terrace.

SCHENECTADY.—*The Mountebanks* of Union College. Russell L. Greenman, president.

SCARSDALE.—*Wayside Players.*

SENECA FALLS.—*Dramatic Club* of Mynderse Academy.

SPRING VALLEY.—*Lyceum Entertainers,* 14 John Street. LeRoy L. Quick.

SYRACUSE.—*Community Players, Little Theatre.* 704 E. Fayette Street.

TOTTENVILLE, S. I.—*Unity Dramatic Society,* 7255 Amboy Road. John Meehan Bullwinkel, secretary.

TROY.—*The Box and Candle Dramatic Club* of Russell Sage College.

TROY.—*Dramatic Society of Emma Willard School.*

TROY.—*Ilium Dramatic Club.*

TROY.—*Masque of Troy.* George A. Luther, secretary.

TUCKAHOE.—*Eastchester Players.*

UTICA.—*American Legion Players,* 233 Genese Street.

UTICA.—*Westminster Players,* care Dr. F. M. Miller, 293 Genesee Street.

UTICA.—*Players' Club,* Mandeville Street. Frank Stirling, director; Miss A. C. Dimon, 1411 Genese Street, secretary.

WARNER.—*Warner Players.* Miss Ethel K. Cox, president.

WATERVLIET.—*The St. Bridget's Dramatic Club.*

WEST POINT.—*Dramatic Society,* United States Military Academy.

WHITE PLAINS.—*Fireside Players,* Inc., White Plains Meeting House. Natalie Harris, director.

YONKERS.—*Sekondi Players.* Marian E. Lee, director.

YONKERS.—*Little Theatre Group,* 24 Wolffe Street. Edmund J. Kennedy, secretary.

YONKERS.—*Little Theatre.* O. Hemsley Winfield director.

NORTH CAROLINA.

AHOSKIE.—*Ahoskie Dramatic Club.* Miss Eleanor Chappell, director.

ASHEVILLE.—*Asheville Dramatic Association.* Edna Phillips, director.

ASHEVILLE.—*Southern Workshop.* Laura Plonk, director.

CARY.—*Cary Dramatic Club.* Lucy Cobb, director.

CHAPEL HILL.—*The Carolina Playmakers.* F. H. Koch, director.

CHAPEL HILL.—*Setzer Club.* Nellie Graves, director.

CHARLOTTE.—*Central Players* of Central High School, East Avenue. Sue Ethel Rea, director.

CONWAY.—*Conway High School Dramatic Club.* Mrs. T. R. Everett, director.

DURHAM.—*Durham Community Theatre.*

FAYETTEVILLE.—*Fayetteville Dramatic Association.* Effie Newton, director.

GREENSBORO.—*Greensboro Dramatic Club.* W. R. Wunsch, director.

GREENSBORO.—*Greensboro College Dramatic Club.* Elba Henninger, director.

GUILDFORD COLLEGE.—*Guildford College Dramatic Council,* Guildford College. Hedwig Hoffman, director.

HAYS.—*Mount View Dramatic Club.* Kate F. Absher, director.

HENDERSONVILLE.—*Hendersonville Dramatic Club,* High School. Rebecca Crowder, director.

HICKORY.—*Hickory Players.* Mrs. E. B. Menzies, director.

HOBGOOD.—*Hobgood Community Players.* A. G. Bowden, director.

HUNTERSVILLE.—*Huntersville Dramatic Club.* Carrie Smith, director.

MOUNT PLEASANT.—*Mont Amoena Dramatic Club.* Clara Sullivan, director.

MURFREESBORO.—*Chowan College Dramatic Club.* Sarah Gertrude Knott, director.

NORTH WILKESBORO.—*Wilkes Community Players.* Kate F. Absher, director.

OXFORD.—*Merry-Makers,* Oxford College. Elsie H. Graham, director.

OXFORD.—*Oxford Dramatic Club.* Ida Michiels, director.

PAW CREEK.—*Paw Creek Dramatic Club.* Fay Choate, director.

RAEFORD.—*Raeford Dramatic Club.* Marthena Bivins, director.

RALEIGH.—*Peace Institute Dramatic Club.* Miriam Everts, director.

RALEIGH.—*The Woman's Club Players.* Corinne Doles, director.

RALEIGH.—*Raleigh Community Players,* 307 Fayetteville Street. Dr. R. P. Noble, secretary.

RAMSEUR.—*Ramseur Dramatic Club.* Carolyn Crawford, director.

RANDLEMAN.—*Randleman Dramatic Club.* Martha Lewis, director.

REIDSVILLE.—*Reidsville Dramatic Club.* Pauline Whieley, director.

SEABOARD.—*Seaboard Dramatic Club.* Bernice Kelly, director.

SPRING HOPE.—*Pershing Players.* J. E. McLean, director.

STATESVILLE.—*Mitchell College Dramatic Club.* Miss C. B. Vaughn, director.

WILKESBORO.—*Wilkesboro Dramatic Club.* T. E. Story, director.

WINDSOR.—*Red Cross Theatre,* Granville Street. Mrs. Francis D. Winston, director.

WINSTON-SALEM.—*Winston Hi Players.* Leonard Huggins, director.

YOUNGSVILLE.—*Racket-Raisers.* Laura Winston, director.

NORTH DAKOTA.

FARGO.—*Fargo Little Country Theatre.*

HAMILTON.—*Community Theatre Building.* Hollis E. Page, manager.

OHIO.

AKRON.—*Civic Drama Association,* Akron Players.

CINCINNATI.—*Garret Players,* Cincinnati Conservatory of Music, Mount Auburn. Margaret L. Spaulding, director.

CINCINNATI.—*Cincinnati Art Theatre,* East Third Street, between Walnut and Main Streets.

CLEVELAND.—*Shaker Village Players,* Coventry and Weymouth Roads. Mrs. William S. Cochran, director.

CLEVELAND.—*The Playhouse,* Inc., Cedar Avenue and 73rd Street.

CLEVELAND.—*The Orations.*

CLEVELAND.—*Library Players,* care Mrs. Ina Roberts, Public Library.

COLUMBUS.—*Senior Class of Grand View High School.* Dorcas Truckmiller, director.

COLUMBUS.—*Players' Club, Playhouse.* 470 Capitol Street. Stokes McCune, director.

DAYTON.—*The R. E. Fallout Players,* 649 Oark Street.

DAYTON.—*Roosevelt Players,* Roosevelt High School, 3rd and Mathison Streets. Bertha May Johns, director.

DELAWARE.—*Ohio Wesleyan University.* Prof. R. C. Hunter, secretary.

EAST LIVERPOOL.—*Gibbons Club.* John Rogers, director.

GRANVILLE.—*Denison University Masquers.* Miss Elizabeth Folger, secretary.

LIMA.—*Ye Merrie Players.*

MIAMISBURG.—*Town Players,* 525 Park Avenue. R. G. Berchier, secretary.

MIAMISBURG.—*Columbia Players,* 304 S. Second Street. Charles Brassington, secretary.

NORWOOD.—*Norwood Players,* Norwood Federation Clubhouse, Ashland Avenue.

NORWOOD.—*Community Players of Ft. Thomas and Norwood.* William Harrison, director.

PLAIN CITY.—*K. of P. Dramatic Club.* Ney S. Fleck, secretary.

PORTSMOUTH.—*Little Theatre,* 73 First National Bank Building. Lowell Ames Norris, director.

TOLEDO.—*Boyville Hall,* 618 Superior Street. Lew Williams, director.

OKLAHOMA.

OKLAHOMA CITY.—*Civic Theatre.* Mrs. LeRoy T. Tryon, director.

SHAWNEE.—*Dramatic Club of O. B. U.,* High School Auditorium. Mrs. Rhetta M. Dorland, director.

TULSA.—*Little Theatre Players.* Mrs. P. Reed, secretary, 1448 S. Denver Avenue.

TULSA.—*Little Theatre Players,* 309 W. 11th Street. Mrs. J. P. Bowen, secretary.

OREGON.

GRASS VALLEY.—*Little Theatre.* C. M. Plylor, secretary.

PORTLAND.—*Portland Players,* 214 Couch Building. K. Eastham and R. Nufer, managers.

SALEM.—*Little Theatre Club,* 193 N. Commercial Street. D. H. Talmadge, secretary.

SILVERTON.—*Silverton Playmakers.*

PENNSYLVANIA.

BUTLER.—*Little Theatre Group,* 245 S. Main Street. J. Earl Kaufman, secretary.

ERIE.—*Erie Little Theatre.*

ERIE.—*Community Playhouse.* Henry B. Vincent, director.

GERMANTOWN.—*Philadelphia Belfrey Club of Germantown Academy.*

GLEN ROCK.—*American Legion Players.* J. B. Koller, director.

INDIANA.—*State Normal School Players.* Edna Lee Sprowls, director.

LATROBE.—*Play and Players' Club.* Ray B. Johnston, president.

LOCK HAVEN.—*Lock Haven Community Service,* 123 Bellefonte Avenue. S. W. Wolf, executive secretary.

PHILADELPHIA.—*University Dramatic Club,* College Hall, University of Pa. Mary Montague.

PHILADELPHIA.—*Philomathean Society* of the University of Pennsylvania.

PHILADELPHIA.—*Three Arts Players.*

PHILADELPHIA.—*Philadelphia Little Theatre.*

PHILADELPHIA.—*Plays and Players,* 1714 Delancey Street.

PHILADELPHIA.—*The Delphian Players,* 1330 N. Alden Street. Frank C. Minster.

PHILADELPHIA.—*Echo Dramatic Club,* 1330 N. Alden Street. Frank C. Minster, director.

PITTSBURG.—*West Liberty Jr. Boosters,* South Hills. Calvin B. Fetteroff, director.

PITTSBURG.—*Red Masquers,* Duquesne University Auditorium.

PITTSBURG.—*Pitt Players,* University of Pittsburgh.

PITTSBURG.—*Department of Drama* in the Theatre of the College of Fine Arts. Carnegie Institute of Technology.

PITTSBURG.—*Temple Players,* 2303 Murray Avenue. L. Robin Secretary.

READING.—*The Community Players.* Mrs. A. Lyons, 414 N. 25th Street.

SHAMOKIN DAM.—*Shamokin Dam School.* H. E. Culp.

STATE COLLEGE.—*The Penn State Players,* 134 S. Gill Street. A. C. Cloetingh, director.

SWARTHMORE.—*The Mary Lyon School.* Helen Loomis James, director.

TITUSVILLE.—*Titusville Little Theatre.*

RHODE ISLAND.

PAWTUCKET.—*Pawtucket Community Theatre.*

PROVIDENCE.—*Brown University Dramatic Society.*

PROVIDENCE.—*The Players, Talma Studios,* 160 S. Main Street. John Hutchinson Cady, secretary.

PROVIDENCE.—*The Komians,* Women's College in Brown University. Sarah Michin Barker, director.

PROVIDENCE.—*Pyramid Players,* Little Theatre Guild of Providence College.

SOUTH CAROLINA.

COLUMBIA.—*Town Theatre.* Daniel A. Reed, director.

WARE SHOALS.—*Y. M. C. A. Theatre.* J. D. Brown, director.

SOUTH DAKOTA.

MITCHELL.—*Dramatic Society.* D. W. College of Mitchell.

SIOUX FALLS. *Dramatic League.*

VERMILION.—*University of S. D.* Professor C. E. Lyon, secretary.

TENNESSEE.

CHATTANOOGA.—*Little Theatre of Chattanooga.* Clayton B. Hunter, business manager.

JOHNSON CITY.—*Little Theatre Guild,* care Appalachian Publishers. Mary Gump, director.

MEMPHIS.—*Memphis Little Theatre.* Colin Campbell Clements, director.

NASHVILLE.—*Little Theatre Guild,* Hillsboro Theatre. Lark Taylor, director.

TEXAS.

ARLINGTON.—*Little Theatre,* N. Texas Agricultural College. Helen Bothwell, director.

AUSTIN.—*Austin Community Players,* 2208 Guadalupe Street. Morton Brown, secretary.

BEAUMONT.—*Beaumont Little Theatre,* 2210 Calder Avenue. Mme Maria Ascarra, director.

BELTON.—*The Protagonists,* Baylor College. Mary E. Latimer, director.

BONHAM.—*Pied Piper Players.*

BRYAN.—*The Little Theatre of Bryan.* Mrs. Paul Stevens, director.

CLEBURNE.—*Cleburne Little Theatre.*

COMMERCE.—*Commerce Community Theatre.* Maud Webster, director.

CORPUS CHRISTI.—*Corpus Christi Players.* 1411 Chaparral Street. Marie Marion Barnett, director.

DALLAS.—*Little Theatre.* Oliver Hinsdell, director.

DENISON.—*Denison Little Theatre.* J. J. Lindsay, director.

DENTON.—*State College for Women.* Prof. H. E. Wilson, director.

FT. WORTH.—*T. C. U. Dramatic Club,* Texas Christian University. Lew D. Fallis, director.

FT. WORTH.—*Little Theatre of Fort Worth,* 609 W. Fourth Street. Hunter Gardner, director.

GAINESVILLE.—*Little Theatre.* Porter H. Wilson, secretary.

GALVESTON.—*Little Theatre.* Peter A. Vincent.

GALVESTON.—*Community Players,* 2215½ Avenue D.

GEORGETOWN.—*Mask and Wig Club.* 1403 S. Elm Street. W. Dwight Wentz, secretary.

HOUSTON.—*Columbia Players.*

LUBBOCK.—*Lubbock Little Theatre.* Mrs. W. D. Green, director.

OAK CLIFF.—*Oak Cliff Little Theatre.* 410 North Bishop Avenue.

PARIS.—*Little Theatre Players.*

PHARR.—*Valley Little Theatre.*

SAN JUAN.—*Little Theatre.* A. A. Martyn, director. Box 73.

SAN ANTONIO.—*Little Theatre.*

WACO.—*Little Theatre of Baylor University.* Sara Lowrey, director.

WICHITA FALLS.—*Little Theatre Players.* Mrs. T. A. Hicks, president.

UTAH.

SALT LAKE CITY.—*Engineering Society,* University of Utah.

VERMONT.

BARRE.—*Senior Class of Goddard Seminary.* Miss Morse, director.
RANDOLPH.—*Chandler Music Hall.* E. T. Salisbury, director.
ST. JOHNSBURY.—*Little Theatre,* 13 Boynton Avenue. Madeline I. Randall, secretary.

VIRGINIA.

CHARLOTTESVILLE.—*Virginia Players,* University of Virginia.
FORT HUMPHREYS.—*Essayon Dramatic Club.* Major Carey H. Brown, director.
HOLLINS.—*Hollins Theatre.* Hollins College.
LYNCHBURG.—*Little Theatre Assembly Hall,* 409 Washington Street. Margaret D. Christian.
NEWPORT NEWS.—*Drama Circle of Woman's Club.* Mrs. Paul Malm, director.
PORTSMOUTH.—*Three Arts Club.* W. T. A. Haynes, Jn., secretary.
RICHMOND.—*Little Theatre League.* R. G. Butcher.
RICHMOND.—*Richmond Players,* 208 E. Main Street. Thomas Nelson Bland, secretary.
SCOTTSVILLE.—*Scottsville Players.* J. F. Dorrier, secretary.
TAYLORSTOWN.—*Little Theatre,* Red Men's Hall. Edmonia H. Baker, secretary.

WASHINGTON.

HOQUIAM.—*Hoquiam Community Players.*
SEATTLE.—*Seattle Repertory Theatre.*
SEATTLE.—*Cornish Players.* Mr. and Mrs. Burton W. James, directors.
SEATTLE.—*Seattle Theatre Guild.*
SEATTLE.—*Dramatic Society,* University of Washington.
SPOKANE.—*American Association of University Women,* Drama League Playhouse. Ann Reely, director.
TACOMA.—*Tacoma Little Theatre,* 620 N. First Street. Mrs. Carl Morissee, secretary, 3007 N. 29th Street.

WEST VIRGINIA.

CHARLESTON.—*Sunset Theatre.* T. M. Elliott, manager, Box 91 Station B.
CHARLESTON.—*Kanawha Players,* High School Auditorium. Mrs. Hunter McClintic, secretary.
HUNTINGTON.—*Neighbourhood Players,* 1016 Sixth.
HUNTINGTON.—*Huntington Community Players,* City Hall, Ian Forbes, director.
WHEELING.—*Little Theatre,* care Dr. Clara Sullivan, 1216 Eoff Street.

WISCONSIN.

APPLETON.—*Sunset Players,* Lawrence College.

BELOIT.—*United Players.* 1417 Portland Avenue. H. D. Ball, director.

JANESVILLE.—*Girl Reserves of Y. W. C. A.* W. A. Munn, director.

MILWAUKEE.—*Mountebanks,* Downer College.

WYOMING.

LARAMIE.—University of Wyoming.

CANADA.

LONDON.—*Western University Players' Club..*

NEW WESTMINSTER, B.C.—*Little Theatre Association,* Room 5, Hart Block. H. Norman Lidster.

OTTAWA, ONTARIO.—*The University Women's Club* of Ottawa Ladies' College.

OTTAWA, ONT.—*Ottawa Drama League.* T. D. de Blois, secretary-treasurer.

REGINA, SASK.—*Regina Little Theatre Society,* 2717 Victoria Avenue. Mrs. G. R. Chetwynd, secretary.

TORONTO, ONTARIO.—*Hart House Theatre,* University of Toronto. Walter Sinclair, director.

TORONTO, ONTARIO.—*The Little Theatre Upstairs,* West side of Yonge Street. Mrs. Franka Morland-Davies, director.

TORONTO, ONTARIO.—*Margaret Eaton Theatre.* Bertram Forsyth, director.

VANCOUVER, B.C.—*Vancouver Little Theatre Association,* 542 Howe Street. Mrs. E. A. Woodward, secretary.

VICTORIA, B.C.—*B. C. Dramatic Society,* Fell Building, 637 Fort Street. Major L. Bullock-Webster, director.

WINNIPEG, MANITOBA.—*Community Players of Winnipeg,* 959 Main Street. Hilda Hessor, chairman.

WINNEPEG, MANITOBA.—*University of Manitoba Players,* 1212 Wellington Crescent. J. W. Russell, secretary.

CPSIA information can be obtained
at www.ICGtesting.com
Printed in the USA
LVOW11s0936070517

533590LV00001B/286/P

9 781417 907496